JT and T:

Connect with
Lee —

You will love
him.

To awesome friends

:) Maryanne

CONTENTS

INTRODUCTION

Think Like a Fan is about how organizational leaders can use resources around them to build a community-based culture of fans that are loyal to their brand. It's about utilizing your existing "fan base" to exponentially expand reach and ultimately create new revenue streams. It's about rethinking how you communicate in the current digital landscape and amplifying what you are saying so that people don't just hear but also listen and respond to the message.

What do you call the people who do business with you? Are they consumers, patrons, customers, clients, etc.? I have become fond of referring to these people as fans. In reality, anyone who does business with you, whether it is monetarily or through trade, is making an investment in your brand and company. **The physical transaction between a person and business may make them a literal consumer; however the choice to put their trust, faith, and loyalty into what you provide makes them a fan.**

Fans come in many forms: casual, fair weather, and die-hard, to name a few. Simply taking money from these people is no longer the most effective business model. With today's limitless connectivity and ability to communicate, cultivating relationships and making these fans feel like part of your organization can be infinitely more beneficial—both monetarily and mentally—than ever before.

In a time when challenging the status quo has become the status quo, consumers have placed a responsibility on all organizations to stand out in order to gain their loyalty, not just their money. The surge of technology in recent years has connected all of us more than at any point in history. Ten years ago, we watched sports on a screen in our home; now we can watch, discuss, and read from a screen that fits in our pockets. In addition, it seems like every few months everyone is jumping on a new app or social site. Today's connectivity has also opened the door for organizations to stay in touch with an audience 24/7/365. Fans are constantly calling for a better overall experience—how are you answering the call? This book is an opportunity for you to create your own unique voice in the marketplace.

Take advantage of opportunities to transform your product from "merchandise" people buy to a "mission" they believe in. For example, your organization can:

- "Broadcast" uniform information across multiple platforms
- Speak with your audience, not at your audience
- Enable current customers and followers to promote your brand
- Stay constantly visible to supporters in order to stay relevant
- Continually "tap" your audience to engage and incite interaction

- Understand how to respond to both positive and negative reviews
- Substantiate internal sales forces to increase creativity and productivity
- Establish trust and authenticity as a keystone of the brand
- Create a digital community that followers want to visit
- Utilize social media platforms to your maximum potential
- Work with (not against) competitors to maximize profits
- Create a culture of confidence in your brand

Many understand that changes are essential but question when might be the right time. The time is now and *Think Like A Fan* is your starting point.

THE PURPOSE OF THIS BOOK

The ultimate purpose of this book is to assist business owners, corporate executives, team owners, marketers, and managers to engage and expand their audience and in turn, their bottom line. Whether you work in an office, arena, or at home, this guide will help you to rethink your approach to communication in order to create a "fan" culture that will grow your overall business.

Think Like a Fan is a mindset and foundation that you can build on and expand to find the unrealized revenue potential and market share for your business that is just sitting there, begging to be tapped. This is your playbook and plan to a business model that you can adopt to remain relevant to your fan base and marketplace. Sports teams thrive and win by formulating strategies, and then executing the next play—on a field or rink that is constantly changing. Your communications and engagement strategy is no different. Outside your office, an infinite number of fans are watching your organization's every move. Even casual onlookers, whether they are in person or through the web, begin developing an opinion of your brand with the slightest amount of information or publicity. With the currently available social connection technologies, individuals are eager to let you know their opinion through comments and other forms of communication. They will not hesitate to let you know what they think you should be doing as an organization, team, or company. It's a never-ending process in which nothing less than 100% perfection is expected. Preparation to lead your fans' community is key, especially in today's fast evolving technological landscape. With preparation top of mind, the tactics and stories we share in this book are based on real experiences, and have all been tested within several types of organizations with the same result—predictable and unprecedented success.

If you have been asking yourself "How do I take my organization to the next level?" learning to *think like a fan* is the answer!

THE FUTURE IS NOW

I have always been in awe of the successful individual's ability to lead all aspects of a business, from managing a work force to creating an internal culture that people can believe in—while maintaining finances, outward appearances, and results. It's a never-ending process that calls upon a person's passion, experience, and courage. While certainly game-changers in your own right, elite men and women like you have paved the way for what is to come.

In order to find continued success moving forward, organizational leaders will all need an improved understanding of how digital technology is reshaping media consumption. Our entire market is integrating deeper and deeper into wireless, mobile, and digital solutions that consumers crave. These innovations create major opportunities for revenue and brand building, if implemented and integrated correctly. Proper planning and preparation for a digital migration effort is essential, and business leaders will find they cannot sit back and "see how it plays out" as they may have with earlier, more traditional marketing methods.

In the coming years, organizations must learn to utilize their existing fan base as their best "sales force." Growing a franchise's fan community on the web, and encouraging communication through multiple mediums including social media, video, and other interactive digital platforms will create more exposure and word-of-mouth promotion than has ever existed. Business leaders often have only a partial understanding of how this can take place. Establishing a strategy that spans multiple platforms will become a vital part of organizations moving forward. In order to accomplish this, teams will need to assemble a hybrid group of professionals that have experience across several skill sets: media production, sales and marketing, business management, and creative design.

There is no doubt that a digital migration is happening. The question most of the business elite are trying to answer is when to make the change . . . and the answer is now, as in *right now*.

Let's get started.

CHAPTER 1

Embrace Change

When you look to the future, do you see all the potential brought on by emerging technology? I am naturally a positive thinker, but that's not the reason why I see opportunities everywhere I look. Take a minute to consider the luxuries we are afforded due to current technology. We live in a time where we can instantly communicate with any single person or group of people face-to-face on a screen, without worrying about long-distance phone charges. We can channel-surf over an ocean of niche networks, whereas before we stayed "close to shore" with the traditional broadcast channels. We can tailor our own incoming and outgoing digital newsfeeds to our interests, and have it accessible wherever Internet is available. **We live in a time with unlimited access to information; unfortunately most are too lazy, uninformed, or fearful to fully utilize it.**

It is a recurring theme throughout history that technology evolves faster than our ability to adapt. In the civil war, weapon technology was far more advanced than the military tactics of the time. As a result, brave soldiers from both sides were often ordered to march across open areas directly into gun and cannon fire. At that time, underutilizing the available technology was a matter of life and death for individuals—today, understanding and utilizing technology is a matter of life and death for your organization.

When it comes to the field of communication and engagement, most individuals know that change is happening and that they need to adapt; the problem is they just don't know how or even where to start. The first step is to consider altering your understanding of what change is, to gain a clear perspective.

CHANGE IS OPPORTUNITY

We no longer live in a time where the next "it" way of promoting or communication will last for more than a few years (months in some cases). Learning to "go with the flow" is becoming a skill in itself. I spent two years of my life convincing small-to-medium-size businesses that having an online presence was vital in today's marketplace. In the beginning, I approached business people with the assumption that they understood the power of the web and would welcome new ideas. The reality was the opposite. Many business owners, executives, and decision makers didn't fully understand the web, and dedicating the time to adapt took a leap of faith.

It was then that I recognized that empowering individuals and business teams to confidently step into the digital realm would allow them to see how digital platforms could greatly expand their current objectives and maximize their business strategies.

My presentations and consulting sessions went from 90% products, services, and benefits-focused to 90% information, history, and education. I committed myself to educating my clients on the changes that were happening with technology in the digital world, and then following up with ideas on how to utilize that technology. The results were exponential in terms of new business as well as success for my clients.

Throughout this book we will explore varied ways to embrace technology and implement it in your current life and work plans. The motivation to learn comes with the knowledge of what's in it for you and those around you. My goal is to create a desire to learn and gain new perspectives through understanding that the online world is a living community. We live in a time with exciting possibilities and tremendous opportunity for you and your business. Your success will be defined by each individual consumer's experience with your company. This is why you must *think like a fan.*

In order to make the transition towards upgrading to the powerful use of readily available technology, the challenge is to rethink how to "sell" and "promote" your products. Gaining the consumers' trust and having a personal connection with them is more important than ever, regardless of your industry.

Will you take the simple challenge to modify your life and work style to be successful moving forward? If you are a visionary leading from behind a desk, move closer to the action without losing your personality, but rather showcase your expertise. If you are in the midst of the action already, ask for input from your customers about their experiences with your company. Additionally, ask employees internally on the ground floor how they feel about your services and company as a whole. Make sure you are *listening* to them, not just hearing them.

EMBRACE THE TECHNOLOGY

Perhaps the biggest changes happening culturally are the digital methods of communication. Digital technology evolves faster and more frequently than any other technological medium we have experienced throughout history. It is due to this fact that many find themselves falling behind the digital revolution and playing catch up today.

> In order to have a true "voice" in the digital age, we must understand the medium beyond its last innovation.

Stay with me here; I will explain.

Simply put, falling behind with your customers and employees in regard to digital technology can be as detrimental as a sports team not providing an athlete with the best equipment possible. They may be able to perform, but not as well as other teams in the league. Keeping this metaphor in mind, athletes will need time to test and use the equipment before they will be able to use it to its full potential.

For example, one the most pressing technological issues today is creating an infrastructure that provides reliable wireless Internet services to handle the demands of a large crowd. Every time I experience a public venue without the ability to connect to the Internet I cringe at the thought of how much revenue is being lost.

A study conducted by GMR Marketing in February 2012 shows that fans are extremely socially involved at sports venues with 63% of fans checking updates while at a game. Think about the potential of harnessing this traffic. Consider how often you see people on their device while at your place of business. Multiply this if you have a brand with multiple stores, outlets, and other customer gathering places.

Levi Stadium in Santa Clara, California, home of the San Francisco 49ers, features "an impressive technological infrastructure that enables high-speed mobile connectivity," according to Sports Illustrated writer Ryan Glasspeigel. The stadium features an app that allows fans to check the waiting lines at food and beer vendors, and subsequently which bathroom has the shortest wait. The Wi-Fi connection in the stadium is strong enough to allow fans to stream NFL Redzone (the Leagues' live game day highlights channel) from their seat, and/or surf the web.

The technological wonder also enticed major sponsorship from a global Internet leader (Yahoo), who was recently named the official sponsor for online sports content, social networking, and photo/video sharing. The company, which is a pillar of the fantasy sports world, proudly put its name on the stadium's "Yahoo! Fantasy Football Lounge." The company also leads digital efforts including installing Flickr-branded photo-sharing booths throughout the concourse, along with other perks for fans.

One of my first major realizations for the potential of "connected" venues came during the 2012 NHL Winter

Classic in Philadelphia when the hometown Flyers took on the New York Rangers. The uniqueness of the event alone (an ice rink on a baseball field) is worth posting about for fans and followers. When I picked up my smartphone I was shocked to realize that I couldn't get enough signal to do anything—not even text. Immediately I was struck by how much marketing potential was being overlooked. Even though the event was being broadcast on TV nationally, the NHL, Flyers, and Rangers had missed out on the opportunity to have 80,000 paying fans connect with countless other people to share the event. The exponential value was incalculable.

Today, many venues are rushing to implementing adequate Internet access into their facilities. In addition, many are seeking out third party app and program developers to help create "second screen" experiences so that fans can interact with each other and the team in the arena/venue during live events. Those venues chasing these ideas will lead the pack into what will become an augmented "fan" experience of the future.

In this new world, no quick fixes or short cuts to understanding the ever-changing digital world exist. Skipping steps or rushing to a conclusion will not supply answers. Like athletes, when the game is on the line, those that stay calm in the face of adversity find the clarity to make the big play. Consider where you might need to clearly understand digital technology shifts for your business segment.

As people migrate towards digital devices, companies will have to be right in the mix of front-end technology to retain consumers' business. We are rapidly heading towards a time period where traditional marketing methods are becoming passé.

Let me say that another way: it's do-or-die time if you want to keep your customers satisfied with your products and services. While companies are willing to jump from medium to medium to stay in front of clients, they often try to re-create the tactics that have been profitable in the past. For example, let's look at the tactic "bending the truth."

While "bending" or "exaggerating" the truth may continue to be a tactic in the future for some companies, modern marketing is slowly taking a major turn towards engaging potential customers and encouraging honest interaction. Instead of assuming what consumers want after conducting market research studies, companies now have the ability to simply ask the socially engaged public directly—companies just need to be willing to listen.

Fully embracing technology will allow your business to create a hybrid strategy that spans multiple platforms. It also spawns the need for a new form of hybrid employee that has experience across several professions such as media production, sales and marketing, business management, and creative design.

Of course, in order to fully embrace anything we must first understand it.

In 2013, I was invited to a meeting with the ownership and senior staff of the Peterborough Phantoms Professional Ice Hockey organization in England. The question that was unsettling to the owners and management was, "How do we increase attendance?" The team had suffered several losing seasons in a row and ticket revenue for each game was starting to dwindle.

In professional and semi-professional sports, we always seem to think that team owners are rolling in dough when it comes to revenue and pay. With a few exceptions, this is largely untrue. A team franchise is a business and, like any business, there are expenses—LOTS of expenses. Aside from paying out player contracts, teams also need to pay for employees, equipment, food, travel, facility charges (rental, maintenance), and marketing, among many other monetary overhead demands. The truth of the system is this: after every ticket is counted and every game is played, teams are lucky if they break even. Since attendance is the number one means of revenue for most professional sports teams (the NFL is the only exception with their colossal TV contract), below par attendance (about 40% of capacity) for the Phantoms was becoming alarming.

The question went around the table and then landed on me, "How can you increase attendance?" I responded, "We aren't the ones who will increase attendance; our existing fans will do it for us." There was silence. It felt like that moment when you hold your breath when the ball is soaring through the air right before it is caught or dropped.

"How are you going to get them to do that? We are near the bottom of the league and they are already getting fed up with the team." I looked the questioning party right in the eye. "When they stop talking about the

Phantoms all together . . . that is when I would be worried." There were nods of agreement around the table. "These fans are some of the most passionate I have ever seen. No one can promote this team better than they can. We just need them to believe in what this team stands for, and they will spread the word. Winning definitely helps bring people into the stadium, but it's not the primary driving force behind the team's success." I knew what the next question would be, "How are you going to do that?"

I smiled, "*We* are going to create a community, and it starts in this room right now with each of us." The meeting continued for several hours after that. By the end of the season, the Peterborough Phantoms saw a 40% increase in attendance, record-breaking interaction between the club and fans, and a completely refreshed brand persona. All this was accomplished during a season in which the team finished second to last and missed the playoffs.

The way the club communicated both externally and internally changed over the course of the season. When it comes to the sports and business world, change can sometimes be the toughest pill to swallow. Rear Admiral Grace Hopper, a former U.S. Naval officer and early computer programmer once said, "The most dangerous phrase in the English language is 'we've always done it this way.'" During my first three months with the Phantoms, my media team and I heard that phrase from the fans more than any other. In time the phrase turned into, "We love what the team is doing."

The toughest part of creating change is knowing where to start. When it comes to changing how you communicate, it starts with realizing that "the way we have always done it" is not the way we do it anymore.

IN REVIEW

- Technology is always changing how we communicate, work, and live. Learn to embrace these changes and not shy away from them.

- There is major exponential value and profits within digital technology for the organization that takes the time to learn, grow, and evolve.

- Get in the game! Change is continuous so never get caught being a spectator.

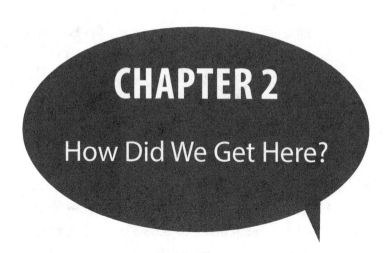

CHAPTER 2

How Did We Get Here?

As a business leader, I understand that you must always be forward thinking, to prevent getting stuck in a moment or set in a certain way of thinking. Almost in contrast to this, we all understand that history often repeats itself.

Have a clear understanding of the difference between reliving the past and knowing your history. Reliving the past can result in holding you back while learning history gains you knowledge—and just like we were all told as children—knowledge is power.

In this chapter, we will touch on the important moments and changes that have taken place in the history of digital media. Knowing the progression of the digital timeline can give lots of perspective on where your business communication structure may be and where it is going. You may find in this chapter that you were unknowingly focused on changes that were important years ago. Don't panic if you are. Simply continue to follow the timeline and understand there is nothing but opportunity moving forward. We all need to learn to walk before we run.

Knowing this history is also important for how you decide to approach your audience. While your fan base may vary in age and demographics, you never want to be in a position where they are saying that you "just don't get it" or that "you are behind the times." Consumers expect you to be up to date and will dismiss you if you're not.

An understanding of where digital media has come from is important to knowing where it is going. **Whether this is a refresher course or your first time learning about the roots of the digital business, know that many of the innovations of tomorrow were inspired by the advancements of yesterday.**

In the beginning there was the web.

After several precursors, the Internet as we know it was born. Originating on October 29, 1969, the (then called) ARPANET (which would change its name to Internet after 1974) was used for the purpose of computer-to-computer communication. Within 25 years of its inception, the Internet was introduced to the public as a means to gain information about news and sports, and to retrieve a new paperless parcel message known as e-mail.

Then came websites.

Shortly after the introduction of the Internet to the masses, websites (which originated in 1991) quickly became a business necessity for most companies. It might be tough to remember, but in the mid-90s if a corporation had a flashy website, it was a cutting edge attribute for their business. As consumers, we would ask, "Do you have a website?" and then give that company an imaginary seal of approval when the answer was, "Yes."

And then came the search engine.

Around the same time the Internet was gaining its initial traction within the household in 1997, two students at Stanford University—Larry Page and Dr. Sergey Brin, Ph. D.—were working on a new Internet program that they called Google. Their new search engine would index and organize websites into a searchable database for users. In 1997, search engines existed online via providers like AOL and Prodigy, and through stand-alone sites like webcrawler. com and infoseek.com. Page and Brin's Google would soon redefine how searches are done. Before Google's formal launch in 1998, only nineteen search engines existed compared to the forty plus that exist today.

Consumers at the start of the 21st century stopped asking, "Do you have a website?" and started saying, "I'll Google you." Having a website was almost immediately expected of most businesses and having that website found on a search engine was significant.

The rise of Google caused large businesses to see massive potential in both online queries and the user's ability to "search" for their products and services. A new process called Search Engine Optimization (SEO for short—the process of organizing the content of one's website to appease the relevancy criteria of search engines) is the new "it" word with top-level marketing executives. Small-to-medium businesses see this as an added expense and largely ignore SEO at this time, still opting for local print and trade publications.

Accelerating the fundamentals of online searching, Google introduced "AdWords" to the search engine in 2000. The new function allowed businesses the opportunity to enter into a bidding process to guarantee first-page placement bordering the normal results on the top, right and bottom of the page. Using a process that demands equilibrium between three sources—users, businesses, and Google itself—the small start-up company quickly became the preferred starting point to surf the web as well as an alternative to the phonebook for people searching for business headings.

Media then became Social.

In 2004, at select universities in the United States, a new website emerged called "The Facebook." The platform quickly grew over a three year period to become not only one of the most popular digital communication services on the Internet, but also began rivaling Google for the most visited site on the web. As a result of the network's popularity, several other "social" platforms emerge. New networks such as Twitter, Instagram, and Reddit among others helped to coin the phrase "social media."

By 2008, Facebook opened its membership to anyone thirteen and older with a valid email address. Businesses began to see the potential in this groundbreaking new enigma titled "social media" as a new way to approach prospective customers. Facebook also saw the potential and soon offered business organizations the ability to create a "business page" for their fans to follow their brands and services on the social site. Fans who "Like" their page can receive updates and participate in promotions. It allows companies a new way to broadcast "press releases" in a social fashion directly to their audience instead of having to go through mainstream media.

And at the same time phones became smart.

In a generation and a marketplace that seeks streamlining and simplicity, the birth of the smartphone was inevitable, and a shining example of how multiple digital devices converged into one: cell phone, camera, calculator, gaming console, audio player, and personal organizer. These devices continued to evolve via trial and error with the consumer, adding and removing features, until Apple mastered the formula with the iPhone.

The rise of the iPhone would also kick off one of the greatest modern capitalistic ventures of the early 21st century. Within two years, flip phones became a relic, as they could not compete with the compatibility and exceptionally advanced functionality of the iPhone. The existing "smartphones" of the time paled in comparison to this new age product, and several companies (Sony Ericsson, Nokia, LG, Palm) went under or were bought out as a result. In spite of their failure, Google (Android), Blackberry, and Windows all created signature smartphone products to rival the iPhone. These players go head-to-head each year on a continued quest to perfect the technology. It is that competition that allows the advancement of the devices and technology to apparently move at light speed.

Within a year of the initial release of the iPhone—amidst its raving success—Apple made a decision that would turn smartphones from a "wish list" gadget into an essential device that would rethink how we use the Internet and become an essential part of the general population's day-to-day life.

And so we entered an age of apps.

Within months of its initial launch, applications (apps for short) were created in a myriad of categories. Among these were smartphone-sized programs that tracked fantasy teams, provided news and sports information, and interactive games. Apple even managed to catch the lightning in a bottle in their famous, "There's an app for that" commercials; the phrase is still used today.

During the rise of applications, and the rise of digital devices during the late 2000's, consumers began to transition from a PC/desktop world to a mobile world. Suddenly, you could carry the Internet with you in your pocket, and consumers loved it. The web was changing from a privilege to a necessity.

By the end of August 2008, large businesses saw the need to create applications and mobile-ready information to satisfy their consumers' needs. Having a business app was slowly becoming a legitimizer in the market place, just as having a website was a legitimizer in the early days of the Internet. Moreover, from a company standpoint, a branded app became a way for the consumer to have a link to a business entity in their pocket 24/7. Small-to-medium size businesses were starting to see consumers use smartphones in their stores more and more. It was an optimistic time for business. However, focus would quickly be shifted from cutting edge technology to mere survival by late September of 2008.

But then, the economy fell.

On September 16, 2008, failures at some of the biggest financial institutions in the USA caused the largest global market crash in history. During the following years, small, medium, and large businesses that had thrived for decades were sold or shut down completely. Consumers began to save money instead of spend it. Contrary to these consumer trends, Apple experienced iPhone sales that more than doubled in the three years that followed. Sales were reported at 11.42 million in 2008, then jumped to 24.89 million in 2009, to 46.6 million in 2010, to 89.26 million in 2011. In the midst of the Great Recession, Apple continued to see exponential sales growth. How was that possible?

The crash of 2008 marked a major moment in our history of digital media. In the years that followed, financial strife, unemployment, and new media resulted in major changes in consumer behavior. Unbeknownst to many business owners, more and more consumers were opting to go online to shop instead of going out.

Just like business owners, consumers found themselves strapped for cash and struggling as a result of the recession. This forced many to find new avenues to save as much as possible. More than ever during this time period, consumers were searching online. According to Statistic Brain, in 2007, searches on Google averaged 1.2 trillion per day. By 2011, that number had tripled to 4.7 trillion. The world is becoming more and more tech savvy and turning to sites like Google to find answers over traditional means. The rise of smartphones and apps only put that practice into overdrive as consumers could now compare prices and products in the palm of their hand while in the store itself. Within a three-year period, consumers went through a metamorphosis that would forever change buying behavior.

Unfortunately, not many small-to-medium business owners of this time educated themselves on this change. While they were aware of the evolving medium of "digital marketing", it was grouped in the same bucket as traditional media and viewed as an "additional" expense. They failed to see that the consumer who recently emerged from the cocoon created by the recession was now equipped with a smartphone and e-commerce experience.

Large businesses recognized the change immediately. Sports organizations rushed to create or update their existing apps with sponsored schedules, video, and content to satisfy consumer needs. The modern sports fan was now craving content on demand, and sports teams were all trying to answer the call. The mantra was simple at this time, "Give the consumers what they want!"

By 2012, the potential for Internet-based advertising for business was apparent, but sadly not operating at full capacity. While the recession had brought users to a starting point for extreme digital interaction, local businesses, which needed to seek out digital advertising formats, were still largely sitting on the fence.

Online Video then became mainstream.

Ask yourself, "What is the second largest search engine after Google?" You might guess Yahoo, right? Surprisingly enough, the answer is YouTube. Following Google's purchase of YouTube in September of 2006 for $1.6 billion (in Google stock), the video-sharing website saw unprecedented growth, expanding from one country (USA) to eighteen countries by the end of 2007, and 58 countries by 2013. With the rise of smartphones and digital devices, video sharing through social media became a common practice among the digital generation. As a result, the stats that YouTube now produces are almost unfathomable; 100 plus hours of video is uploaded to YouTube every minute, 25% of YouTube views are on a mobile phone (1 billion+ a day), and YouTube uploads more video in two months than the combined programming of NBC, ABC, and CBS since ABC's first broadcast in 1948!

Hoping to capitalize on the platform's global success, YouTube utilized an advertising strategy similar to Google AdWords, and pay-per-click advertising. In December 2010 YouTube launched "TrueView," a behaviorally based advertising platform in which users would see video advertisements tailored to their interests before selected videos. Business owners who pay to make sure they are seen in front of their prescribed audience were only required to pay YouTube if a user clicked on the ad or watched it for more than thirty seconds.

Then the mobile market expanded even more . . .

In April of 2010, Apple once again redefined the market with the release of a new mobile device, the iPad. Although not the first tablet ever created, the keyboard-less, touch-based device allowed people to surf the web, read books, download apps, take and share photos, and use applications on a large mobile screen.

With the market flooded with mobile devices, coupled with an increased need from consumers to have mobile-ready content, many websites went through a transformation, creating mobile-ready "responsive" websites that could conform to whatever shape or size tablet or smartphone the consumer was using. This factor, which is an extreme legitimizer today, along with the impending crossover of mobile devices dominating PCs begs the question, "Which is a more important asset: my desktop website or my mobile website?" While large organizations have already conformed to creating mobile-ready content, small-to-medium businesses are still slowly finding their footing.

Then we all went into the cloud.

In October of 2011, Apple introduced iCloud, a service that allows users to backup and store data from their computing devices (PC/Mac computers, iPhone, and iPad) to an online storage center. Although Apple wasn't first to the cloud market, the launch of iCloud made the concept of "cloud storage" mainstream.

Instead of having to constantly link your devices to a computer to update and sync, all the information can be uploaded and downloaded wirelessly. Many users are realizing that they no longer need to buy books or movies unless they want to. One can simply download them and have them on standby with the cloud. Magazines and podcasts download automatically to your online digital media center.

Cloud technology has drastically accelerated the ability for our devices to interact. Computers can correspond with smartphones, tablets, entertainment systems, and other items wirelessly and automatically. In addition and for the first time, businesses can share files with employees who can access them from any device with an Internet connection, allowing for increased productivity. The cloud made file sharing a near instant process, 24/7.

Throughout the history of the web, technology transformed and evolved the medium several times and will continue to do so as we move forward. Some of the innovations increased users while others changed how people fundamentally experienced the web. While no one can predict with 100% certainty when and where the next digital innovations will come from, if this history teaches anything, it's that consumers and businesses embrace the technology and do not hesitate to interact when given the chance.

> Perhaps the greatest advancement as a result of the events in digital history is the development of the digital voice that everyone—including businesses, groups, and people—now has.

More importantly is that, no matter which aforementioned category you belong to, your online voice is on an equal wavelength with everyone else.

It is because of this leveling of the playing field that how we communicate has also transformed—and as a result, how you do business needs to go through a digital transformation. We are all now part of an online community and your goal is now to become a leading voice within that society.

IN REVIEW

- Knowing the history of the digital medium will help give you perspective on where your business's communication may currently be and where it is going.

- Many of today's advancements and innovations were inspired by inventions of yesterday. Understanding them can help you blueprint the future.

- The most prominent advancement of the digital revolution was the creation of a digital voice that every person, business, and entity now have the ability to use.

CHAPTER 3

Speak With, Not At Your Audience

You as a leader know that your organization needs to continually change and adapt to the current digitized landscape that has become a cultural immersion. This digital transformation is not as daunting a task as you may think. Implementing and launching new strategies is a fun and exciting process once you are comfortable with the digital approach. That is the easy part. The hard part is first learning to migrate from traditional methods to new.

Old school marketing is based on advertisements and companies reaching out to consumers, and is measured by sales. New school marketing is based on communication between consumers and companies, and is measured by loyalty. Don't worry, I'm not going to try and convince you that profits are not important; they are extremely important. What I am going to do is convince you that putting fan loyalty ahead of your bottom line will exponentially grow profits.

Traditional methods are creative in nature, meaning that advertisers try to find and attract consumers. Usually done via billboard, print ad, radio and/or TV commercial, these ads are only as powerful as its relevancy to the consumer that may or may not be driving by, watching, or reading. These methods result in one-directional communication from the business to consumer via advertisements. The goal is simply to inform and move on. This gives companies an aura of speaking "at" viewers. Marketing techniques such as these can be enhanced when companies make ads more interactive by asking for feedback and questions. This helps to create a two-way dialogue between the business and consumer, but maintains a line of separation when communicating.

Validating the time and money spent on traditional advertising is simple. If consumers buy more products and the company makes more money because of the ad, it's worth the cost. Traditional marketing methods still work but their value is rapidly dwindling within today's marketplace. Have you noticed in recent years more blank billboards than actual billboard ads? Have you noticed that print editions of newspapers and magazines are being inundated with advertising in place of articles? As the traditional method is based largely on the "chance" the engaged public is interested, the time has come to start re-thinking how much of your marketing budget gets invested in them. These techniques still have value, but only if the cost is justified by adequate return on investment.

The web has provided us with hundreds of communication platforms and has made them available across multiple digital devices (phones, tablets, computers, etc.). Trying to go through each option is overwhelming. That may be the number one reason people get deterred from utilizing them. The constant in the digital social realm is that everyone has the opportunity to speak with anyone else on an equal playing field. The trick to new marketing is not to pick and choose which platforms are the best for your business; it's to create a message, a mission, and an identity that surrounds your brand—one that people can believe in—and then share it with the masses by any means possible. **The ability to speak *with* your faithful followers and not *at* them (as was the traditional method) is of paramount importance to be successful in the new market place.**

Modern marketing is all about inciting communication and driving interaction by creating content. Let me define content in the digital world: anything and everything about your business or industry that you feel is in good taste to share with the public. Don't get caught up in the mindset that "nobody cares about what we do." It's not true. If John Deere can get over 325,000 views on a YouTube video titled, "How to Pattern Mow Your Lawn," you can get your audience involved with information regarding your business! We will explain more about how to utilize content in different forms later in the book. **For now understand that content is your key to touching your fan base.**

Likes, follows, shares, searches, and reposts equal dollars today. It is easy to see why many people view social media (Facebook, Twitter, Instagram, Pinterest, etc.) and content interaction platforms (blogs, websites, Reddit, etc.) as a popularity contest. Digital outlets are your opportunity to play the role of keynote speaker at a convention where everyone attending is interested in what you do, and then follow it up with breakout sessions where you get to meet the people you were speaking to.

These methods of communication operate under a three-way process that incorporates communication from businesses to people, people to businesses, and people to each other. Now that consumers can speak to other consumers, opinions and perception matter more than ever before. Individuals now have a voice and they use it. Because of this,

> it is important to respect your audience as an equal partner when pushing out information. Don't treat them like consumers; treat them like fans. Find their pulse and mimic it back to them. You are now in a personal relationship with them, not just a business partnership.

This was the fundamental ideal for revitalizing the Peterborough Phantoms fan base. If you had spoken to Phantoms fans prior to the year I came on board, they would have conveyed a lot of pride in being a fan of the team, told you about the organization's glory years in the early 90s and the mid-2000s, and followed it all up with a complaint about how the team is being run today. We set out to change that mindset.

We began to reach out to the fans on the Phantoms group Facebook page with our own personal profiles—

not a generic one for the team. I wanted people to be able to put a face to my name and know they could reach out to me whenever they wished. Once I had established myself as a member of the management team, I created fan surveys giving the Phantoms faithful the opportunity to sound off. I wanted them to KNOW we were listening to them. Sometimes just the perception that you are listening is enough—but *knowing* is even more powerful! At the same time, I created content for the fans, such as a game promotional poster with the team logo and text that read, "Meet me at the Phantoms game!" I then asked them to share the photo and tag friends in it. I also provided online Q&A sessions with the players. This was a fan favorite as they were able to digitally connect directly to the players.

Using feedback we received from the fans, we completely revamped PeterboroughPhantoms.com (now GoPhantoms.co.uk) to better serve our fans' needs. We also created a new fan-run supporters group aptly called "Phanforce," in addition to a rewards-based incentive campaign for fans who bring new people into the arena. Both ventures were very successful overall, creating spikes in revenue, attendance figures, and sponsorships sold. In addition to the above, we also ran several themed events (holiday parties, kids contests, military appreciation, etc.) on game nights in addition to many other in-game improvements. Results were immediate and reverberated throughout the season.

Although these efforts were made through intangible digital means, it was very tangible to the fans; the connection was real. Finally, and perhaps most importantly, I responded to every comment and question that I could on the Phantoms' social media channels. I was speaking directly *with* them.

This had a dramatic effect in turning the polarity of emotion from negative ("THEY don't listen and they don't care about US") to positive ("We may not be doing so well but WE are moving in the right direction"). The fans had become a part of the team and the team a part of the fans.

Above all, when speaking with fans I committed to being as human as possible. When questions were asked, I gave a straight answer. When mistakes were found, I acknowledged and thanked the appropriate parties and made the adjustment. This "real" connection is what your fans crave.

IN REVIEW

- Begin the process of evolving into more modern methods of marketing and communication in order to start the framework of building your brand's digital presence.

- Create an overall message and mission for your business that an audience will be proud of and be able to connect with.

- See your consumers not just as customers, but as your biggest fans.

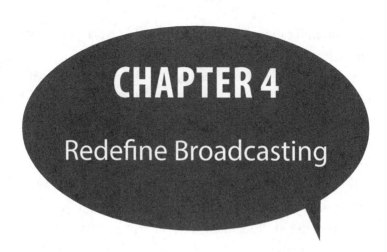

CHAPTER 4

Redefine Broadcasting

We are all broadcasters today. Whether you communicate as yourself or as a business entity—what you say can be sent to potentially thousands if not millions of people across the globe via the digital channels that now exist. Traditionally, the word "broadcasting" encompassed communicating content through television and radio. With the emergence of social media, smart phones, and other breakthrough digital technologies like the cloud, broadcasting content can now be achieved by anyone—24/7—across a continuously growing number of platforms. In the age of information, companies now have the opportunity to broadcast personalized content to a specific audience globally, and it's critical they learn to do so.

> The ability to broadcast today is a necessity in order to stay relevant in the eyes of your fan base.

Communication took on new meaning when the radio and television became mainstays of the home. Using the power of electricity and waves in the sky, networks began to show news, shows, commercials, and anything else that viewers would watch. The term "broadcasting" was created and turned into one of the most important and profitable mediums in the history. By early 2013, the Interactive Advertising Bureau (IAB) reported that approximately $40.1 billion was spent advertising on broadcast television alone.

A traditional "broadcast day" consisted of having to choose programs from a variety of channels on the TV or radio dial. Viewers would plan their day in order to catch certain programming and had little to no choice or control over what shows or advertisements would come and go. Over time, more channels were created—giving the audience more options to choose from—but still little to no control over what programming would be on. In the early 2000s, computer and digital technology began to enter the "broadcast" world with streaming content and recordable devices. Suddenly, one could record his/her favorite shows and choose exactly when to watch them— but still, the viewer had little to no control over what was being presented.

It was with the emergence and rapid evolution of both modern digital technology and social media in the mid-2000s that the element of "choice" within broadcasting changed. For the first time, with the emergence of texting, video, and photo sharing, and other means, anyone (not just broadcast networks) could upload and share their own content with a niche audience at their chosen time across multiple platforms. With the new ability to create personalized content, every person, business, and organization was given the ability to "broadcast" their own personalized news, shows, content, and information. Even advertisers could now target their audience based on location and behavior. With that, the money started flowing in. By the end of 2013, the IAB reported that approximately $42.8 billion was spent on digital/online media, surpassing broadcast television for the first time. This statistic shows that advertisers feel that consumer's use of online media is more beneficial than advertising on TV. Moving forward this scale will only tilt more in the same direction.

Consider what is happening now in today's digitally connected marketplace. The opportunity for organizations to "broadcast" has created the opening to clutch success in the local, national, and even global marketplace. It is safe to say that your audience craves content. Now more than ever you can create and implement campaigns to broadcast your brand and message to the masses.

When I joined the Phantoms organization, the team's existing fans, although very loyal, were very critical of the organization and the team; a negative attitude surrounded the club. After I took a good look at the organization, I realized that their social media platforms were highly underused, and the management and staff were critically disconnected from the fan base. The current fans operated as almost a separate entity from the team, resulting in a disjointed fan community, and a negative and stagnant aura surrounded the brand—both of which were incongruous with the mission and vision of the organization.

The franchise needed to begin broadcasting to the masses as a whole in addition to uniting its workforce internally. As a team, we began to create highly interactive, opinion-based content across our digital social channels daily to make fans feel more involved. Once that was accomplished, we encouraged our fans to invite new people into the arena and gave them tools, resources, and incentives to do so. We created a new Phantoms Hockey Community that revolved entirely around the team and broadcasted the content they craved daily. Whether it be a sound bite and/or interviews from games and practice, sharable photos and posters, live on-line Q&A sessions, or many other interactive activities, our fan base responded by communicating and sharing the content for us. It was not long before there was a "buzz" on the street about us.

After a tremendous amount of planning, hard work, and collaboration with some great co-workers, we were able to turn one of the most pessimistic fan bases from negative to positive, and increase attendance over one year by 40%. Team revenue reached the black for the first time in several seasons, despite the team placing second to last in the league that season. The team also saw 50-100% increases in followers on the team's various social media accounts. The momentum built from my first year with the team transitioned beautifully into the off-season as we continued to broadcast player signings and other related content. With a foundation now in place, the team can continue to use this formula to be successful year after year.

Most organizations understand the need to utilize the many different communication methods at their disposal over the Internet and through our digital devices. What may not be fully understood is exactly how and what to broadcast over these channels. Before putting any campaigns into place, a business must understand this new approach to broadcasting.

IN REVIEW

- Broadcasting today encompasses traditional mediums like TV and radio in addition to social media, digital video, websites, blogs, and many more online services 24/7/365.

- Companies must broadcast engaging content such as news, photos, video, blogs, discussion based forums, promotions, and more across multiple mediums in order to be seen as relevant to their fan base.

- Your audience craves engaging and interesting content – create and provide it for them and watch them share, discuss and debate all while speaking about your brand.

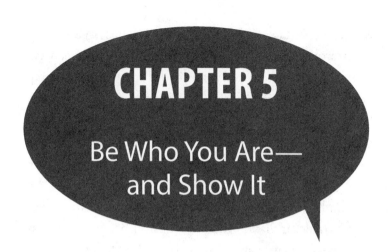

CHAPTER 5

Be Who You Are—and Show It

In 2013, Microsoft entered the tablet market with the release of the "Surface." Available in two options, the basic RT model and the PRO model which included a stronger processor, additional digital storage space and a larger resolution screen. In addition to being the first mainstream tablet with a USB port, both versions of the tablet ran a full version of Windows 8. The Surface also came with a flexible keyboard that doubled as a screen cover. In short, the Microsoft Surface was the first mobile device capable of fully replicating the experience of a laptop or PC in tablet form.

When it came time to begin advertising the Surface, Microsoft's largest competitor was predictably Apple and the immensely popular iPad. Coming into 2013, iPad had a powerful 60% market share over the tablet market. Hoping to differentiate them from the iPad and appear unique, Microsoft created an ad campaign called "The Vibe."

The commercial starts in an office interior, a conference room where a bunch of young employees are sitting around a table. Ready to work, one of the executives activates his

Microsoft Surface tablet. He pulls out a pen stylus as the other around the room open their Surface tablets as well. Almost immediately everyone in the room begins to tap pens and their screens, creating a musical beat. In between beats we see Office-like applications appear on the surface tablets such as Windows 8, Microsoft Excel, and Netflix. As we move around the room, attendees break into interpretive dance using their tablet as an accessory. Within seconds, we see employees dancing on the boardroom table with their surface tablet in hand. The now musical beat continues as the party turns into a full break dance. Suddenly, an upper executive walks into the room with an assistant. The room freezes. The assistant plugs a microphone into the surface tablet he is carrying and begins to freestyle beat box while the upper executive begins to break dance. Immediately, the room joins in. In groove, the upper executive uses a stylus pen to put a large check mark on the screen of an employee's tablet. The dancing continues and escalates to more intricate moves before culminating in a final beat. We then see, "introducing the Surface Tablet" followed by the Microsoft logo.

This ultimately failed to connect to an audience. While the ad has a dramatic flare in addition to an entertaining concept, it barely informs the viewer about the basic practicality of the Surface. In July of 2013, Microsoft reported a loss of $900 million due to lackluster sales of the Surface RT model (the simpler of two versions created). The result was a 30%+ price drop after it was revealed that marketing costs exceeded sales.

The ad's failure is rooted in focusing on competing and differentiating themselves from competitor products (mainly the Apple iPad) rather than focusing on communicating with their consumer. Instead of announcing loudly that Microsoft had entered the tablet market, the group should have showcased the elements of the product that made it a stand-out necessity in the digital marketplace for any demographic looking for a tablet-computer. In the end, Microsoft morphed their advertising efforts for the tablet towards more of an informative theme—and sales followed.

Now that we are all deep into the information age, consumers are not just looking for the newest, flashiest goods. They are becoming more and more educated about the ins and outs of every product and business in which they choose to invest their money—from the coffee they drink in the morning, to the store they stop at for groceries, to the TV or digital device they consume media on every night. This begs the question: in a world where everyone is communicating around you, how do you get their attention?

AUTHENTICITY

How well do you know your fan base? Really think about that question. Do you know what it is about your products or service that they love and dislike? Do you know what age and gender demographics they come from? Do you know what is popular within those demographics right now? Do you know what social platforms they use? Do you know what times during the day and week they are most likely to be searching for you?

Now imagine if that question was reversed; how well does your fan base know you? Do they know the backstory of your organization? Do they know the day-in, day-out operations of your business? Do they know leaders and other individuals that work for you? Why do they classify you as unique? Are they aware of the full potential that your business has to offer them?

In the past, answers to questions like these may have been classified as "non-pertinent." Today these answers are essential to establishing the authenticity and trust needed in order to build true loyalty, and **loyalty is the highest denomination of social currency in the marketplace.**

Use this equation on a personal level. Who are your most trusted confidants? Why do you trust them? Your answer to that question is most likely based on specific situations and personal experiences with those people. Earning someone's trust starts from your first encounter and is as simple as providing exactly what you are claiming to offer whether it be friendship, product or service. **The process of legitimizing that trust is called authenticity. In simpler terms—be real with people, most notably those who will be your fans and customers.**

> The authentic brand speaks with its audience, not at its audience.

This is why it is so important to know your fan base and that they know you. You cannot effectively "speak" to someone that doesn't have anything in common with you. I often hear in the advertising world that companies must "create a need" for their audience, meaning make a reason for them to spend their money with you. I challenge you to rethink what the word "need" means. **Strive to be better than simply creating a generic need for what you are providing; instead create a need for your brand to be essential in a consumer's life.** When that is established, people will promote your business for you.

In order to start establishing an authentic approach, begin by answering these questions as sincerely as possible:

- What motivates you to get up each morning?
- What do you love about where you work and why?
- What is unique about your brand or organization?
- What are you passionate about as a professional?
- What sets your workplace apart from others?
- What do you love about the people you work with?
- What do you love about your fan base?
- Name three interesting things about your day-to-day operations that people outside the organization aren't aware of?

Questions like these provide the answer to what makes you authentic. The answers are also some of the first things you should share when engaging your audience. This can be done via writing a blog post (you can literally title it "Why We Exist") or sharing a photo that represents one of your answers (such as a visual representation of what motivates you) with a short description. Even something as small as creating an open ended social media post that says something along the lines of, "Aside from having breakfast, having the chance to make a difference in people's lives motivates us to get up each morning. What motivates you?"

> Speaking to people on a personal level will help you touch their heart instead of just their wallet.

The beauty of today's expanded communication platform is that we can constantly tap our fans through the day/week/month/year. Many make the mistake of providing product information at every opportunity. The consumer has a word for this: spam or in laymen's terms, "junk."

Whether you are preparing to communicate digitally, through traditional print, or over the TV or radio, make sure you broadcast in a way that will relate to your audience—your fans will appreciate it.

Share something that your audience can connect with in addition to images of your product. A good rule of thumb when creating sharable media for social media and other digital means is to have 75% of your content not specific to your products and services.

All businesses, from plumbers to professional sports teams, have an audience that is interested in what they do. If they didn't, there would be no demand for what they are selling.

The Internet is an infinite source of information worth sharing. Find and provide insightful and interesting information for your audience about your industry. Your willingness to educate your fan base will be greatly appreciated by your audience while promoting your brand at the same time.

In addition to information, don't be afraid to share general thoughts. If it's a nice day, take a photo and share. If you see something that is funny (and in good taste), share. In addition to sharing, you can write messages to engage your audience. *(We will give many more specific, examples in chapter 10.)*

Another great option is to share praise that you receive from your fan base. If someone sends you a note or photo endorsing your product, share it on your social media platforms and website and then encourage others to send you more. This method helps to show that you care about your consumers while simultaneously promoting your business.

At the end of the day, companies are always looking for a way to be unique for their audience. Authenticity is the ultimate way to stand out. Just like people, every business is a bit different. Explore your organization from within. **Define what your company identity is and share it proudly with the masses.**

TRUST

As part of being authentic, organizations must adopt the best practice of being truthful regardless of the situation. As consumers now have the ability to speak and influence each other when it comes to information, being dishonest can ruin a reputation faster than ever before.

When we think about relationships, whether personal, friendship, family, or business—trust should be the keystone they are based on. Trust establishes the bond that companies should now be striving for with their audience. In addition, organizations should seek to work with other partners that share the same ideal of trust.

Only when trust is earned can two parties begin to grow and evolve to build the most powerful element of a relationship, loyalty. Loyalty creates return clients, referrals, and many other benefits. There will be times when something inevitably goes wrong, and quick action will be needed. Never compromise the trust of your relationships, even in the face of this adversity. Take a step back, confer with your media team and colleagues and figure out a way to work the problem; weather the storm. Create an honest response and explain to your audience the best you can what went wrong and your plan to fix it. If trust is lost, the entire house can come crashing down.

Implementing this ideal may be easier for some companies than others. It starts with taking a good look at your company from within and seeing what kind of trust atmosphere exists already. Do your employees trust the company? **Establish an internal trust environment before portraying yourself as a trustworthy company to the masses; you can't give them something you don't already have.** Once that is accomplished, you can begin to approach the people.

I was first brought in as a marketing consultant with Hockey WrapAround, a company that created a protector for the bottom of ice hockey sticks, in the summer of 2014. During the first six months of its existence, the company saw massive growth on the popular photo-sharing site Instagram. As a young company, client referrals and praise were tremendously important to both spreading the brand's name and convincing people to invest in the product. One evening, the company was tagged in a photo of a broken WrapAround with a less than desirable sarcastic caption that was being shared by an account with over 20,000 followers. The account that shared the photo had recently bought a WrapAround and it had broken within 24 hours of use. The photo of the broken WrapAround quickly gained traction through social media; negative comments were shared on both our pages and the person's who originally posted the broken unit.

While many within the organization panicked, I viewed the situation as an opportunity to reach out to both our fans and a potential new follower base. Instead of defending the product (which would have been seen as an excuse by the public), we reached out directly to the user that posted the picture. We first apologized on behalf of the company for their poor experience, and then followed up by asking questions about how he was using the product, as it might be responsible for the break. It was eventually determined that the client had attached the product incorrectly which resulted in the break. Regardless, we offered to send a new blade free of charge—all that was asked in return was for the client to speak publically about his customer experience.

The customer was extremely happy with the WrapAround's response. He agreed and immediately shared a photo to his followers about his experience and newfound confidence in the product. The result was over 100 new followers to the Hockey WrapAround Instagram account within eight hours, and a spike in product sales over a 48-hour period. We stayed in contact with the client over the next week as his new unit arrived. In return, he shared an additional photo using the replacement, captioned with an approving comment that promoted another small spike of followers and orders.

IN REVIEW

- Don't underestimate your audience. With today's unlimited access to information people have the ability to be informed on anything and everything they desire with a click of a button.

- Before you start communicating to the masses, create a loyal and authentic culture within your workplace. You can't give people something you don't already have.

- Trust is the keystone on which authenticity sits. Never compromise it! If you break your followers trust it will be nearly impossible to get it back.

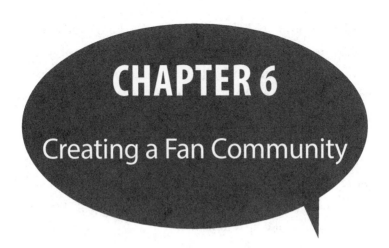

CHAPTER 6

Creating a Fan Community

Now that you have the foundation for a digital voice, how will you use it, and what benefits can you expect?

Before you start "speaking" let's get to know your digital landscape better. As the web comes with countless platforms for brand promotion and interaction with others, it can be hard to know how or where to start. The digital stage is very unpredictable and can seem daunting if you are not familiar with the newest advancements and innovations.

If you want to come across as an authentic company that will earn people's loyalty, you need to deliver more than just staggered status updates and information. By creating a communal experience, your online presence can become a destination that people crave to visit.

The online community is not just a place where people speak; it is a place where people live. We don't just use the Internet anymore; we experience it. We live in a digital world with our family, friends, co-workers, celebrities, businesses, politicians, and literally anyone around the globe that can find an Internet connection. There are no borders or property lines. **Real estate in the online world is limitless; ownership is defined by the size of your audience. In order to build an iconic presence in the digital world, establish yourself as the leader of a community and invite people to join it.**

The beauty of creating an online community is that it can be applied to any digital platform. When the next big player in the social media world is born, you simply need to learn how it works and then apply your message instead of having to make up a new one.

> Establish a consistent, coherent presence and voice for your company online, and people will follow YOU wherever you go. You won't have to chase them.

THE DIGITAL CITY

How you present yourself in the online world is not much different from the real world. Think of the online world as a major city. Within this city live millions of people—all from different backgrounds and different demographics. Some people are single, some have families, some are newlyweds, and some may just be visiting for a time. These people all represent your current and potential audience.

Just like the people, many different types of industry exist in the digital city. Some operate at the top of a glass skyscraper and others are in an old brick store on the corner. Some are well established and some are start-ups. Large or small, you share space in this city with them.

The city's roads and transit options represent the channels for people to find information about you and for you to get information to the people. Some are direct routes, while some are less-traveled roads. Like most transportation systems, you have multiple ways to get where you want to go. Subsequently, there are also rush hours and peak/off-peak times on your information super highway. Knowing how to effectively navigate in any city throughout the day can be the difference between being efficient and disorganized. Furthermore, it can be the difference between road rage and a nice peaceful commute.

Schools and libraries also exist in your city with the purpose of educating the people—just as in real cities, online schools and libraries are beneficial to the digital public as long as they are kept up to date. Educational institutions are often the most underrated part of a community; in the digitally-accessible city, educational and informational resources are valuable. Remember, knowledge is power!

Underneath any city are the power, water, gas, and utility lines that keep it running. These systems are usually out of sight and out of the public mind until one of them fails. Maintaining this utility foundation is vital to preserving people's happiness and security.

Now imagine you are running for mayor of this city. How will you establish yourself as a leader to the people? How do you gain the trust and respect of the city's businesses? How do you utilize the transportation systems within the city and make sure they keep running? What information and education options do you provide to the people? How do you preserve your city's foundation while moving forward?

These are the types of questions to consider before you can feel comfortable with the power of your digital voice. The good news is you don't have to have all the answers to begin. You can create a "campaign staff" for your coming election. Surround yourself with a group of individuals from within your organization that represent your company at varied levels. Recruit the people that will expand your outreach and further your vision—look for inspiration from everyone.

Are you seeing the value of being the mayor/leader/visionary of your fan community?

THE FOUNDATION

Your employees, contractors, and vendors are the foundation of your business. Without them, forward progress simply would not be possible. From your management team to your sales force—make sure that everyone understands the mission and goals you want to achieve. Once clarity is established, cultivate relationships by consistently updating everyone involved on progress. Ask for their input about everything from how to best implement ideas to whether their work environment is conducive to achieving the goal(s). **If your internal staff is engaged in the mission, they will do more to support it.**

THE EDUCATION SYSTEM

Ben Franklin said, "An investment in knowledge pays the best interest." Keep that top of mind when building a fan community. **Educating your audience equips them with the knowledge they need to be powerful and loyal supporters of your brand.** People love to talk about what they know. Equate this to sports fans; there is no bigger claim to fandom than knowing more about your team than anyone else.

> Empower your audience with knowledge of your company and industry, and they will become unflinching, outspoken supporters when given the opportunity.

Start supplying your audience with information about your trade—not just about your specific brand. Get in the habit of sharing important, relevant content regarding your industry. You will become a trusted source of information within your industry to both your fans and other businesses. Find existing blogs, news sources, and publications that lend themselves to establishing you as the information provider and leader. In addition to sharing great daily content, this research will also help you to stay on top of current developments within your industry.

Together with personal background information about your expertise, inform people about company history.

Providing fans with background on the company's beginnings gives them insight and investment into your professional life and story. It also allows them to connect with you wherever they might be in the timeline of life. Share—don't lecture about—your experience with your fans. **We all have to start somewhere; don't underestimate the power of humanizing your organization.**

In addition to connecting with fans, if your organization is well established or has a long-standing history, share nostalgic moments and highlights through photos, blogs, and video. People love seeing timeless or vintage information even if it seems a bit trivial. Content of this nature can become great talking points and stir conversation within your community.

Using the example of educational institutions, preserve information and make it available to your audience. This can be done by creating a historical section on your website, and photo albums or video channels online. Make all content searchable so that people can share it with others or reference it in the future.

THE TRANSPORTATION SYSTEM

Just like a major metropolitan region, your digital city has many transportation options. In the real world this equates to roads, highways, rail, bus, and water transportation options; in the digital world these routes are traveled through search engines, websites, social media, video players, and forums. And like the competition between transportation companies in a real city, multiple companies contend to provide digital denizens with their online information—both for the collection (search engines, websites) and the delivery (desktop computers, laptops, tablets, and mobile devices).

THE LEADER

Your role as mayor is to guide people from wherever they are online to the information you are providing as smoothly as possible. The first step is to establish what message(s) you will send to the public. Being found on Google, liked on Facebook, followed on Twitter, viewed on YouTube, or linked through LinkedIn will not be a priority for potential fans and customers if they aren't relating to and latching on to what you are saying.

Once you have established your message, start conveying it through your website (in addition to listing your products and services, company bio and other pertinent information) and build around that message. Create sharable items such as infographics—videos and written content that support your mission—then begin posting them across the digital networks with a message that entices interaction.

Once you have created this digital presence you can begin to expand. Start to note internally which platforms are bringing fans to you and which aren't. This will give you a good picture of which efforts are working and which may need to be tweaked. Also note which demographics are strong or weak on each platform. For example, your social network's base may be mostly female while another platform may attract predominately young adults aged 15-24. How you convey your information to an 18-year-old heading to college needs to be distinctly different from messaging to a business professional in a different age demographic. Keep the core of your message intact while learning to communicate to different types of people.

If you don't feel confident speaking with a specific demographic, take it as an opportunity to grow and learn.

> The ability to diversify and target business communications to different demographics is a form of social currency.

Create a team from within or outside of your workforce of people with different ages, backgrounds, and genders. Explain your mission and ask open-ended questions that speak to the core values of your message. Make sure to never discuss any assumptions you may have about these demographics—simply ask, listen, and learn. If you wish to take it a step farther, start visiting the popular social channels within each demographic and reference the material they use for inspiration. Just remember to test your content if possible to confirm that you are sending the right message.

Finally, make sure that people know about the many different ways to access your information. Include social media and website badges (the Facebook "f", the Twitter "t"), and website information with everything that you do. To take this to the next level, offer exclusive content on specific channels and invite people to join those platforms to access it.

For example, if you want to drive more traffic to a YouTube page, you can share a still photo on your instagram page with the text "Subscribe to our YouTube channel to see the full video!". While all your digital outlets should share the same core message, how you go about presenting it can be easily modified.

Also, pay attention to other top marketers and companies that have a clear following within a given transportation system (platform). Don't be afraid to find inspiration in what is working for others.

THE INDUSTRIES

Coca-Cola or Pepsi, Apple or Microsoft, McDonalds or Burger King, Nike or Reebok, DC or Marvel, Ferrari or Lamborghini? Did you pick one from each brand pair? Millions of people do everyday. Die-hard fans from every brand will always be sure to let you know why their chosen product is the best. The illusion or implication that they must choose one strengthens this process and gives fans a reason to debate. Regardless whether you are loyal to one, both, or neither, the fact remains that none of these companies would be as profitable or as popular without the other. This competition and the need for fans to pick a side is something that can be re-created and expanded upon online.

Digital media creates the ability for companies to work together online. While competition will always be a part of free commerce, the organizations that choose to work online with other companies within their medium will find there is enough business for everyone. **When using your digital voice, invite other companies to empower**

your mission while also supporting theirs by sharing common content.

To be fair, no one is saying you should find your number one local competitor and snuggle up next to them. However, search out other companies that provide similar products or companies whose services would work well with yours and reach out to them about combining efforts and/or sharing information. If you are trying to build an audience, search out other well-established entities that have a large following and ask if they would be interested in promoting you on their digital pages and/or you promoting them on yours. They may ask for a similar favor, compensation or a free product in return; simply gauge each situation in stride.

In addition to having a friendly relationship with businesses online, you can also stir the pot (in a positive way). Don't be afraid to playfully jest with competitors and opponents. This process invigorates the loyal followers on both sides of the wall and entices them to speak up to defend what they believe in. As long as this tactic is done in good taste, it can be beneficial for all parties.

THE PEOPLE

By far the most important part of any metropolis is its people. The digital plateau has more people in it than any one place on earth, and within that audience are all of the people that follow and are interested in your brand. Like any candidate looking to gain votes, understanding how to win over an audience is everything. **People have many interests; learn to tap into them in order to grab their attention and start earning their loyalty.**

> Your industry's following online is a
> culture—connect with it.

When broadcasting information, speak to the essence of that culture. Explain why you love what you do. Find trending topics within your culture and share them across your digital presence online. Ask your followers what they think. Respond to questions that people are asking about your industry. **Take every opportunity to communicate with those who are passionate about your trade.**

Most importantly, when dealing with people online, understand that communication goes both ways. Social media removes rank or status from each digital voice, and levels the playing field. This is part of its authenticity; use that power to build your own. If a fan comments on something you have posted or asks a question, make sure to respond.

Online communication is equivalent to being in a large room packed with people. If you asked a question or made a comment to someone and they just smiled and walked away without responding, how would you feel? Perhaps more importantly, how would those around you that were watching feel?

> Your best asset when trying to garner new
> fans is your existing fan base.

Earning their loyalty will provide you with a larger sales and promotional force than you ever thought possible.

Apple created one of the most successful global communities, where anyone and everyone is invited to be an active participant. More than just the invitation, Apple created a fun and innovative product line that helped bring people together. If you are an Apple user, soon you may not be able to imagine your life without iCloud. All Apple products (iPhone, iMac, iPad, Apple TV, iPod, etc.) are interconnected through iCloud. The online storage system allows all the aforementioned devices to communicate with each other and share media (music, books, video, apps, etc.) that have been purchased through Apple's online marketplace (iTunes— App Store, iBooks, etc.) wirelessly. All Apple products also receive free operating system updates ensuring that consumers' shared devices are always up to date.

This allows Apple followers to stay connected to their own media library wherever they go via their devices or the Internet. It's a perfect example of a company driving the media convergence forward.

The company could also be credited with supercharging the mobile revolution with the introduction of the iPod, iPhone, and iPad. While Apple's products were genius inventions/innovations, even more brilliant was the marketing surrounding them. The ads were incredibly simple yet told the audience everything they needed to know. Whether it be the original iPod commercial of dancing human silhouettes with illuminated headphones and music player, or the iPhone commercials with one hand swiping and selecting applications—Apple was speaking with everyone—and people loved it.

Today, Apple products are found in every facet of the personal and professional world. Apple is a trendsetter that the entire digital industry uses as a benchmark. Their ability to connect everyone has created a close-knit community in which everyone benefits at various levels. Everyone has a voice and Apple gladly listens and asks for feedback in order to improve their products.

IN REVIEW

- Establish a strong voice and community in the online world and people will naturally gravitate to you to learn more and get involved.

- The digital world just like the real world: full of people, industry, economy, and infrastructure. Learning how these elements work together are essential to building your online community.

- Create a culture online for your business and fan base and communicate wherever opportunities exists in order to grow your community.

CHAPTER 7

Expand Your Sales Force into a Fan Force

I have never really liked the phrase "Sales Force." Defined as *"all the employees of a company whose job is persuading customers to buy their company's products or services,"* the idea of a sales force is an aging concept. Your company's culture can be a place where employees and fans can share an equal hunger to promote your brand. The job of "persuading customers to buy" has evolved into "earning people's trust to gain loyalty." "Products and services" are now "mission and goals." Putting this all together, the new definition for "sales force" becomes: *"all the members of a company's community who build people's trust in order to earn loyalty to the organization's mission and goals."* Let's expand your Sales Force into a Fan Force. **The most powerful way to grow business and expand reach is by empowering your passionate fans to use their voice.**

There is no stronger force for your organization than your existing fan base.

Over 90 percent of consumers trust "earned" media such as word-of-mouth and recommendations from friends and family above all other forms of advertising. Inspire your fans to start spreading the word about your company! Create content that is sharable while inciting interaction. **When loyalty exists, your followers will crave content that speaks to them so they can share and promote your organization.** The trick to championing this technique once again lies in speaking with and not at your faithful. Have fun with your fans and make them feel they are part of your organization. The more they feel accepted the more they will support you publically.

THE STARTING POINT

No matter where your current place is within the online community, utilizing digital media is the fastest way to expand your fan base. Focus on the three main segments of digital media: social media, your website, and digital devices (smartphones, tablets, etc.).

If you have not done so already, begin to invite people to join your existing social platforms.

A majority of consumers are equipped with a digital device connected to the social community; invite them to connect with you.

A great way to do this is in your actual place of business. Offer a discount of some sort as incentive (e.g., "Like our Facebook page and take 5%" off today's order). If you don't work in a physical location, offer the opportunity to "Follow us to receive offers and updates." Do not operate under the assumption that they will automatically join your community. For most, the thought to connect is not top of mind when out and about. (We will present more in-depth social techniques in chapter 10.)

Company websites have long served as a destination for people to find and learn information about your company. In the digital community, your website is your corporate headquarters. It should reflect your company vision and aura, and also offer up to date content and information. Upon arrival, your fans should feel welcomed and either be escorted quickly to the information they are trying to find (with tabs or links clearly labeled), or given the opportunity to explore (with engaging content such as photos, video and featured stories). The easier you make the experience, the more likely people are to come back and share with others.

Taking the time to make sure your website is formatted to show on any digital device (also known as responsive design) is very important to the fan experience you are trying to create. **We all experience the web differently; try your best to cater to everyone by enhancing the user experience regardless of what device they use.** Some prefer to check mail and surf the web on their desktop or laptop while others are completely attached to their mobile device all the time. Take the steps to ensure that all outgoing content is accessible across the digital spectrum.

With fans now being "connected" all the time via their mobile and at-home digital devices, you have the ability to reach out and "tap" them throughout the week. I use the word "tap" specifically. Tapping your fans means to offer information if they are interested without obligation. Like the real world, catching someone's attention strategically is much more powerful that being in their face all the time. Overusing or abusing your ability to reach out to your fan base can turn fans off much like the friend we all have that talks endlessly about themselves and never asks how you are doing. Think of this process as a digital handshake and an offer for people to get to know you a bit better.

CONVERSION

If one were to ask a modern businessperson what the word "conversion" meant, they would most likely respond by saying, "It is when a customer gives us money, and I give them a product." Ask the same question of a modern digital marketing agent and they may say, "When someone buys a product in a store, 'likes' a product, recommends a product, and/or promotes a product online." *Yes*—this is the true meaning of conversion.

A question that I hear often in the world of digital business is "Can traffic on social media be directly linked to sales?" The answer is seldom. However, is that the question organizational leaders should be asking?

Change the question to, "Can the information I provide on social media equate to increased awareness which will lead to sales?" And the answer becomes a resounding "yes."

The engaged fan speaks and responds. The engaged fan promotes and will even defend your company if needed. The engaged fan also provides invaluable feedback about their experience with your company. No matter how many followers you have online, if you are not engaging them, their value to you is greatly diminished. **Engaging your digital fan base is by far the largest opportunity to build loyalty and expand your reach.**

During the second half of the 2013-14 season with the Peterborough Phantoms, we created two new fan development campaigns to help drive new people into our arena for games. The first undertaking was to create a fan-run supporters club. We reached out to some of the Phantoms' more involved fans to gauge interest. Within a month we set up a small board of directors who had several ideas on how to garner membership and create team benefits. The name Phanforce was chosen and we began to tease the fans immediately. We created a simple and brief one-minute video for YouTube, social banners for Facebook and Twitter, and set up an information booth at home games.

In addition to Phanforce we also set out to create a fan rewards incentive titled, "Mission 1000." The concept was simple; we would reward existing fans for bringing new fans into our building. We created tiered reward levels based on how many new fans a person cumulatively brought to a game over a two-month period. Prizes ranged from a signed team picture, signed jerseys, and all the way up to a full season ticket. The additional revenue being recorded from each new fan justified costs. As a bonus, if a new fan came back to a second game, the original sponsor received an extra point to their tally. Finally, to encourage people to join Phanforce, we offered a free point to anyone who became a member of the club during the incentive.

We built up excitement by announcing the incentive during games over the sound system, on social media, and through an explanatory video on our YouTube channel. The Mission 1000 sign-in table was placed immediately past the ticket window for ease and awareness. At the end of the two-month period, for every ten people who signed up, we saw 50 new fans attend. In addition, over 10% of our regular fan base signed up for Phanforce before the end of the season.

IN REVIEW

- Your existing fans are the best resource to supporting and promoting your brand. Cultivate those relationships in order to earn and inspire them to continually endorse you.

- A majority of the online audience has a digital device with them all the time. Make sure to give them the tools to promote you whenever and however they wish.

- Modern conversion is when someone buys a product in a store, likes a product, recommends a product, and/or promotes a product online.

CHAPTER 8

There is No Such Thing as Good Publicity

When people have the ability to talk there is never a shortage of opinions. Twenty years ago, opinions were shared over dinner conversation; today anyone and everyone with an opinion can broadcast it over the web on social media, blogs, review sites, and websites. Offering their thoughts on everything from major management choices to the minutest aspect of your product, people are willing to share their experience—good or bad—with the masses. The cut to the chase idea with this concept is to learn how to maximize the polarity of any situation to benefit your company or organization. Rather than let opinions destroy your reputation and cause a loss of market share, use them as an opportunity to touch your fan base and increase loyalty.

The ability to speak with your audience by responding to public online reviews is one untapped opportunity for increased communication. Realize that you are not just responding to one person, but also everyone reading it.

Not replying to a good review about your business is the equivalent of a young sports fan asking for an autograph from their favorite athlete and being completely ignored. Not replying to a bad review about your business today is the equivalent of ignoring someone screaming, "Rat!" in a crowded restaurant.

> Responding to all reviews, good or bad, is an opportunity for your business in today's digital world.

Responding to a positive review not only says "thank you" to the person who gave the compliment, but also lets readers know that you are listening. Moreover, responding to positive reviews can encourage others to write them. Positive reviews are also very sharable as testimonials for your website and social channels.

Don't make the mistake of only listening to the good and not the bad reviews you receive. While some people share when they enjoy themselves; many more will share a bad experience. The ability to handle undesirable reviews the right way can change the polarity of a situation from negative to positive for the countless visitors that may be reading. **Regardless of whether a post has a good, bad, or indifferent connotation, they are all an opportunity to connect with your fan base on a positive level.**

The first step in learning to respond to negative reviews is to remember that you cannot please everyone. No matter how much experience your work force displays or how tight your quality control may be, things inevitably go wrong.

Some reviews are straight forward and to the point while others are packed with emotion and opinions on how your workflow should operate. Try not to take anything disgruntled people say about your business personally. For all you know, they are just having a bad day and their problem with your service was just the cherry on top. Make sure all negative reviews are approached with an open mind and the motto: "*This person has taken the time to let us know they are unsatisfied and we must do the best we can to assist them.*"

The next step is to actively listen to what they are saying. Pinpoint the root problem of the review; they had a bad experience, something broke, bad customer service, shipping problems, etc. Once the problem is identified you can begin to formulate a response. A great process I learned to follow is to create brief generic responses to each of the above situations (in addition to any others that are common with your business). These generic replies can serve as a guideline and great reference point to begin writing your reply.

Listening to your fans can serve a double purpose. They can give both feedback and valuable research information, but more importantly they let you know how your fan base may be feeling. **It is not always easy to be in touch with your fan base on an emotional level; reviews are your opportunity to connect with them.**

The next step is to actually reply. Whenever starting a reply, make sure to start your response with, "Thank you for taking the time to write," no matter how harsh their review may be. This simple gesture sets a positive tone for both the respondent and any audience that may be reading. Follow the thank you by saying something along the lines of, "we are sorry that you had a bad experience with our product." This acknowledgement tells your audience that you don't think of yourself as infallible. Moreover, you didn't say directly you did anything wrong; you in essence said, "we are only human" to the audience.

Now you are ready to insert your generic response. Keep it simple and be honest. If you are experiencing slow shipping, say so. If they had a bad customer service experience, say that you will be sure to address the problem immediately. Sometimes the best response (especially if they had a bad experience or something broke) is to invite them to "personally contact us through an email or messenger to discuss the issue." Let them know, "we value feedback from our fans as it helps us make a better product." This gesture is a message to your audience that the door is always open to discuss anything.

Following these steps is the difference between your audience thinking that you provide sub-par goods and don't care what they say, to appreciating you for taking the time to acknowledge an issue and respond. You may find that when you respond the right way, other fans may even respond to support and/or defend you.

The final step of the review process is to follow up. A typical outcome to following this process is the reviewer will respond with "thanks" and contact you directly, or simply not message again. Another result can be that the person will write back, still upset about the problem. If you feel you are getting caught in a battle of "he said, she said," don't play the game. Remember—you can't please everyone. If you feel you have made a satisfactory response don't be afraid to say so ("We have done our best to find a solution to your problem and will be glad to discuss it more via email. Thank you again for your time.") and stop responding. In my experience, your audience will most likely realize you are being somewhat harassed and dismiss the person making the negative comment all together.

United Airlines got a taste of how ignoring a complaint can have major repercussions when Canadian musician David Carroll wrote and uploaded an original song depicting his experience on a flight. During a layover in Chicago on his way to Omaha, Carroll overheard from other passengers on the plane that baggage handlers loading the plane were throwing guitars on the tarmac. Upon his arrival he found that his $3,500 Taylor guitar had been broken along the neck.

After nine months of deliberating with the airlines customer service department to no avail, Carroll decided to think outside the box. The musician wrote a very catchy humorous country song titled, "United Breaks Guitars," recorded it with his band "Sons of Maxwell" and uploaded it to YouTube.

The lyrics of the song depict Carroll's experience and culminates with the catchy refrain, "You broke it, you should fix it. You're liable, just admit it. I should've flown with someone else, or gone by car... 'cause United breaks guitars." The song continues on to mention specific people that work for United by name.

The video received 150,000 views during its first day, 5 million its first month, and reached 10 million views by February of 2011. The song was so popular that Carroll

THINK LIKE A FAN

wrote and released two more music videos depicting his guitar saga. All together, the three videos received 16.6 million views.

The result of the song was instant fame for Carroll (the song hit number 1 on iTunes the week after its release) and a public relations nightmare for United. A month after the first songs' release, a spokesman for United did his best to turn the negative incident to a positive by complimenting Carroll, saying United would be using the video for future training and promised that the airline would learn from the incident and change its customer service policy.

IN REVIEW

- Reviews--whether positive or negative--are your opportunity to connect directly with your audience on a personal and public level.

- When you respond to any review, understand that you are not just responding to one person, but also to everyone that reads it.

- Take the time to respond to every review in a professional and polite manner.

CHAPTER 9

There are No Giraffes in Ghana

During the 2014 World Cup, Delta Airlines fell victim to forgetting to do a simple fact check that resulted in viral scrutiny from the online audience. Truly, I am not intending to pick on airline companies, they just happen to provide great examples. The mistake took place following the United States initial 2-1 victory over Ghana in the group stage of the tournament. Following the match, the airline tweeted a photo that showed the final score with a picture of the Statue of Liberty (representing America) on the left side with the number two and a picture of a giraffe (representing Ghana) on the right with a one.

The only problem is that there are no giraffes in Ghana.

Tweeters, bloggers, and even the television news called out Delta on the mistake forcing the airline to remove the tweet and make a public apology. As if things couldn't get worse, the apology tweet said, "We're sorry for our choice of photo in the precious tweet. Best of luck to both teams." Delta quickly deleted the tweet and reposted with the word "previous" to replace the incorrect use of "precious."

The initial mistake, which was most likely an honest error by a social media manager, could have been avoided had they just fact checked their information. The result was a media frenzy calling out the airline. In what was obviously a frantic moment, the airline rushed an apology that was also flawed (and of course caught by the Internet).

We all make honest mistakes; there is nothing wrong with that. Even top publications make the occasional typo and factual mistake. It's when similar mistakes are made multiple times that a company's professionalism may come into question. The smallest slip in your team's media, even if an honest mistake, can come back to bite your business big-time. The incorrect picture or wrong spelling of a word can easily be taken out of context and have repercussions on a large scale.

> The 60 seconds it takes to fact check could save you 60 days of crisis management.

When entering into a modern marketing system, a lot of new content and creativity must be produced. With such an influx of information, it can be easy to forget to check facts. The trick to keep situations like "Giraffes in Ghana" from happening is to take the time to fact check and proofread before you post and broadcast. In short, **establish a culture of accountability in your workplace.**

The most effective team is one that is accountable for their own actions but more importantly for the actions of their team and teammates as a whole. When this mindset exists, you will find that when problems occur, the group will correct the situation on their own without placing blame on others or relying only on a leader. Moreover, within a culture of accountability, repeat mistakes are very rare as the group strives to always be moving forward towards a common goal rather than just meeting the status quo.

When it comes to work being done, your group should always assume that information might be wrong and research, check, and then double check each other's work. It takes minutes and can save you days/months of clean up. **We have unlimited access to infinite information at our fingertips; use it. Teach everyone in the organization how to research and "Google" for information.**

There are many easy ways to quickly check your sources. First and foremost, when it comes to spelling, if there is any doubt at all, simply look at an online dictionary or type the word into a search engine and see what comes up. While doing so, it never hurts to review the definition of a word to make sure it's what you mean to say.

> The hardest type of mishap to prevent is the one you don't know exists.

The solution for this is simple; teach your group to identify assumptions—and question everything—especially if the topic is not your specialty. Take advantage of reputable online resources such as search engines, Wikipedia, and professional journals and make sure your message is correct.

IN REVIEW

- Always take the time to double and triple check your work (such as facts and spelling in blogs or social media posts) in order to avoid potentially minor to catastrophic mistakes that can cripple your reputation.

- Teaching your employees to stay accountable and to research thoroughly before presenting is the best preemptive action a company can take to avoid a crisis situation.

- The hardest type of mishap to prevent is the one you don't know exists. Never assume something is right after the first or even second draft.

CHAPTER 10

"Fangagement"

Easily the best part about sharing the mindset of your customers and fans is the ability to apply it to real world applications. In this chapter we will explore several tactics you should consider when trying to engage and grow your audience. How you choose to utilize these digital assets heavily depends on what you are trying to accomplish, and what kind of company you own or what brand you represent. You may need different strategies and tools at different times and for varying circumstances. The good news is that once you grab the ideas, they are easy to share across multiple social networks and digital devices.

ORIGINAL CONTENT (NEWS STORIES)

The most important application to create when jumping into the digital realm is original news-worthy content. A commonly asked question is, "what is considered news worthy-content?" The answer is anything that would be of interest to your community. New hires, new products, and upcoming sales/events can all work. In addition, writing brief product reviews, Top Ten lists, how-to-guides, and Frequently Asked Questions articles are also great written content that can be shared with your fan base. Think of it as your opportunity to broadcast the news on a station that you own. **Never hesitate to share your expertise and establish yourself as a professional.**

When writing a press release or article, keep it short (3-5 paragraphs or 250-350 words) and make sure it's both interesting and contains everything an audience member needs to know. To add some flavor to the article (never a bad idea), insert a quote from a member of your organization. This is a great way to add a human touch to the article.

Use this as an article or press release guideline:

Paragraph 1: The announcement you are sharing

Paragraph 2: Background information about the announcement

Paragraph 3: Interview of internal figure regarding the announcement (if needed)

Paragraph 4: Interview with person/expert on what the announcement is about

Paragraph 5: Closing statements/where fans can get more information

Once your information is written, decide on a date and time for a digital launch.

> The best way to do this
> is to publish the story, article, or
> release on your website and then post
> across your social media platforms with
> a one line synopsis, and link back to your
> website for the full story.

This tactic funnels fans from your entire social sphere to your website which will help to establish it as your brand's "home base" online. This process is very popular in alerting search engines to your presence in addition to creating a clean, smooth, and unified presentation on the web.

DIGITAL BANNERS

Banners and posters are perhaps the easiest element to create. Luckily for all of us, simplicity is in right now. Flashy images with too much going on are often dismissed in favor of a photo or image with a clever short phrase. It can be something as modest as taking an interesting photo that represents your business or industry and branding it with your insignia (along with social media and website logos). Accompany that with text such as "Like if this photo speaks to you" and put it on Facebook, Instagram and Twitter. Asking your fans to share a post can generate powerful connections.

Depending on your industry, you can also search for a photo that hits the essence of what you do and add a slogan. A sports team might share their logo over a field or arena with the message, "If you need me tonight, I'll be at the game." A plumber may show a leaking faucet with the message, "Nails on a chalkboard to the common person but music to our ears." A department store might show the main concourse of their store with the saying, "I'd rather be shopping." Things like this can be done daily if the creative bug finds your marketing department.

An additional method when using banners is to engage your audience by inviting individuals to be part of the story. Most social media channels allow you to "tag" yourself and others on an image; invite your audience to do that with both questions and challenges.

As an example, when working with Hockey WrapAround, we often connect with our audience through humor by posting a picture of a funny situation, such as a player falling down, and then asking our followers to "tag a friend that needs to practice." Over 500 of our fans tagged a friend within 24 hours, resulting in both some hilarious responses but more importantly a spike that day in new followers. In addition to posts like the above, we also regularly post product updates, short videos, and fan reviews of our product. Overall our posts are probably 70% humor and fun, 25% product-based, and 5% acknowledging holidays and national events. This practice of engaging Hockey WrapAround followers has helped establish the brand and product in the hockey community with engagement and humor rather than traditional straight-forward advertising. It has also been more productive in creating sales while being less expensive than a traditional advertising campaign.

Popular programs such as Microsoft PowerPoint and Keynote (standard with most PC and Apple computers respectfully) are perfect and affordable options to create such items. If you want more advanced editing software, download Photoshop. It's easily the most popular and powerful visual editor on the market. For a tutorial on how to create banners, check out the "Think Like a Fan" section on LeeMJElias.com.

DIGITAL VIDEO

Fans love to view content that is tailored for them, and they love behind-the-scenes invitations to see stuff they can't normally get through national or local media. The ability to engage through written content is powerful, but engaging through visual content can resonate even more with your audience. Think of it this way: you may remember the title of a great book you have read but it might be hard to quote your favorite section. On the flip side, you'll likely remember not only the title, but I'll bet you can give me a quote from your favorite movie if asked. **According to the Social Science Research Center, 65% of those in your audience are visual learners. Additionally, 30% are auditory learners. This encompasses 95% of your audience. This makes video, which encompasses both, the essential means to reaching your audience.**

Whether you are a large publicly traded company on the NYSE or a small startup with almost no budget, you can create your very own niche network via a video-sharing website. Creating your own television network in the past would cost millions; creating your own channel today is as simple as registering through a normal online sign-up procedure on YouTube or Vimeo.

In the past, securing a production crew to produce, film, and edit a short show for television would have cost tens of thousands per episode. Today, at a bare minimum, most people have a basic digital HD video camera on their phone. Investing in editing software for in-house use is also very affordable. Another inexpensive route can be out-sourcing to a local advertising agency or University media department, a more simplified and productive means to deliver live video to your social audiences.

While a cell phone camera and student editor may not be the best options for quality and experience, the point re-mains that anyone who wants to create video content today can. A good rule of thumb for this is as long as it's not pain-ful to watch (due to bad quality, poor camera work, etc.), fans will click play.

Explore the idea of creating a weekly digital lineup of mini-shows (2-5 minutes in length) for your audience. Shows based on topics such as "Meet the Staff," "Behind the Scenes," "Highlights of the week," and "Product Previews/ Reviews" among other formats are simple to create and publish to your media networks. To save time producing, you can even ask your fans to send their videos to you and then choose your favorites to share. Call it "Fan Friday" or something equivalent and watch it become a video destina-tion for your community each week.

Enlist members of your current internal media/market-ing team to brainstorm ideas about how to best produce and implement an air schedule. The format for shows that profile employees, managers, and company leaders is simple. Simply sit the interviewee down, give them a microphone, and have someone ask ten questions (create a nice background to make the experience more enjoyable). Have the show edited (with an opening image and song) and you'll have a nice four-minute webisode ready to go.

For shows that analyze and/or preview upcoming products, approach local media people such as respected journalists and bloggers that follow your industry to jump on board. (Their already-established followers will help you with an additional audience.) If you have the means, choose someone to host your shows. Having a spokesperson can help establish familiarity with your audience and put a face to your organization.

Prior to recording any show, make sure to do a little homework. Research the topic thoroughly and write down talking points or bits of information that really stick out to you.

> Remember, when doing an interview of any type, the answers you get depend on the questions you ask. Consider your fans' point of view and establish questions they will want answered in your show.

Scripting web shows is similar to the process for writing articles or press releases. Above all, make sure that your host or speaker comes across naturally and speaks to the viewer as if they were having a direct conversation. Do your best to have hosts and guests speak directly into the camera.

This creates the illusion that they are speaking directly to the viewer.

Follow this generic guideline when creating your initial lineup of shows:

Intro (5-15 seconds): If possible, create a short opening with title and your logo.

Welcome (0-15 seconds): Host welcome, introduction, and today's topic.

Basic Information (30-60 seconds): Explain topic details or background clearly.

Expert Opinion (1-3 minutes): Be specific and give your thoughts on the topic.

Question (1-3 minutes): Ask questions of your audience and invite interaction.

Close (5-15 seconds): Share brand logo, links to other videos, and ways to contact.

SHARED CONTENT (NEWS FROM THE INDUSTRY)

Similar to press releases and articles from your own organization, take time to find attention-grabbing media shared by other organizations. This shared content can constitute articles, press releases, videos, blogs, photos, or any other type of information created by another reputable source that you can re-post across your platforms.

Not to be confused with plagiarism or copying, "shared" content retains the originators logos and information, or is cited by you when posting (e.g., "Check out this post from Company X regarding recent developments within our industry."). **The value of sharing content from other reputable sources is the ability to help establish you as a destination for interesting news and information from within your industry.**

To make this easy, follow other companies from your industry across social networks and news feeds. Furthermore, begin to follow the top 5-10 bloggers from within your industry. If they post something that is interesting to you, odds are it will also be interesting to the people that follow your business online. As an example, a professional sports franchise might share highlights published by their league (especially if their own team or players are included), in addition to posting their own video highlights each week across social channels.

When sharing a link, make sure to write an engaging post along with it. For example, if you are sharing an informal post that provides specific information about a topic or item, your accompanying post should say something along the lines of "Have you been searching for answers about this item? Click below to see a great article and learn more." If you are sharing highlights or other reviews, be candid. Say, "Just in case you couldn't get enough highlights, here is a great video with some more!" If you have an opinion that is in good taste, feel free to share that but always ask for your readers/viewers opinion as well when writing the post. Make sure to be creative and continue to keep it fresh. Below are some additional examples you can use as a starting point.

Informational re-post: "We found this article very informing. Take a look and let us know what you think!"

Highlight re-post: "Which of these highlights is your favorite?"

Review re-post: "Check out this review from GenericCompany.com on our 'product name.' If you have 'product name' let us know what you think by posting below!"

Inspirational re-post: "We could not agree more with this quote from company X. What are some of your favorite quotes on 'topic x'?"

No matter what you are re-posting, always try to end your text with a question to engage your audience. Asking for their opinion and responding can go a long way in gaining both loyalty and customer feedback.

THE COMPANY BLOG

Blogs differ from news stories in that they read more like a personal diary than an official news story. Think of them as a personal editorial or opinion column. We all have spoken conversations, debates, and discussions every day. Whether it is your own personal blog or a group blog that includes entries from multiple people, blogging is your opportunity to document and share your thoughts from one of those conversations. They give you the ability to write an open letter to your audience on a topic.

When trying to establish yourself as an industry leader, nothing is more high impact than sharing your journey.

In the past, publishing your story would take a book deal and years of memoirs. Today it takes half an hour every few days to put your thoughts down in a Word document, and minutes to upload it to your website where it becomes available to the world.

In addition to engaging an interested public, blogs also keep your business and website relevant to search engines by providing them with fresh content. The Googles, Yahoos, and Bings of the world operate on relevancy and nothing makes you more relevant than new and up-to-date content. Additionally, you can promote your blogs each time they are published across your social networks. Just provide a link to the content and explain in one sentence what your blog is about (e.g., "Want to know more about how Item X was created? Click below to see my most recent blog.").

Along with the content itself, your blog's visibility to search engines can be enhanced in several ways. Using hotlinks (links in your blog post that lead to another website) and including buzzwords that are trending can help to expand your blog's reach. For example, if you are citing another article in your blog, make sure to hyperlink the text that mentions the article, which will direct the reader to the source material in a new tab. In addition to hotlinks, also include appropriate photos and videos if they are available to support your points. Finally, the usage of meta-tags (or just called tags on some websites) allows you to summarize the topic of your blog and select buzzwords for search engines to find, attracting those searching for your topic. These techniques are just part of the overall mix, when earning a search engine's vote of confidence as well as your fans'.

EVENT SHARES

Got an event coming up? Invite your audience. No matter how big or small an upcoming event may be, use the resources at your disposal to get the word out. A commonly made mistake with event shares is timing. Just like a job interview, you don't want your interviewees to show up too early or too late. The kind of event you are having will determine the right time differential to alert your audience. A good rule of thumb is to equate the digital invitation with when you might send a written invitation. Below are a few examples of potential digital event shares.

Facebook event creation: Facebook allows you the option to create an event through your business page. All you need to do is input the information and Facebook will share for you. You can copy and paste the event URL and post as a link on your website and other social networks as well.

Banner creation: Simply create a digital banner that provides the basic information for your event (date, time, highlights, short summary) with some interesting visuals and share across your social networks. If you have a large schedule, such as a sports season or event calendar, in addition to making a full calendar for your viewers, you can create monthly themed versions (with a different player or subject).

YouTube video: This option is also perfect for sports teams or organizations that have lots of events during a season or year. Create a short video that showcases some recent highlights or shares a message that speaks to your cause and place the dates at the end of the video. This option is highly sharable.

In addition to promoting an event invitation, you also have the option to engage your audience by asking them questions about the event and get feedback if desired. Make them feel involved and they will be more likely to attend, and perhaps more importantly, share the event with their friends.

PRODUCT PREVIEWS AND REVIEWS

If your company is a retail-based organization, product previews and reviews are a must. As you work towards becoming a trusted destination for your fan base, product previews and reviews are a service they will look to you to provide. Be sure to answer the call. Your fans will appreciate your providing them with the information and, assuming you sell the product or service, they will know exactly where to go to make the purchase.

Previews and reviews can be done through a video, photos and/or a write up. Using all three of these methods in one article is the optimal way for several reasons. How your fan base accesses the information plays heavily into how they want to consume it. The person accessing the information at home may have time to sit through a video review, while the person on the go might just want to browse quickly and move on. No matter what situation your fan base is in, provide them with multiple means to get the same information.

Ideally, you will want to include several elements when creating a good preview or review. Here are some options:

Written review: When composing the words for a review, it is best to organize the article as simply as possible. Create a section for "positives," "negatives," and "overall thoughts" where you can list any other information you wish. People viewing this information are most likely at the point in the buying process where they are close to making a purchase—make it easy for them.

Video review: Follow the same format as the written review but also include product demonstrations within the video. Seeing a product in action will significantly help the viewer decide if they want to move forward with a purchase or not. Having a host with a video review can be a nice luxury but videos such as these can also been done via a simple voice over.

Photos: Include them throughout the written and video reviews! Provide your fan base with the visuals they want.

Ratings: Finally, when creating reviews on a regular basis, create a star-rating chart of some sort (e.g., 4 out of 5 stars). This tactic is the ultimate quick reference point and when you gain traction as a trusted source for reviews they will become a major part of a person's final decision.

If your company is not retail based, morph creating product and reviews into previews and analysis. For example if you are a sports franchise and you sign a new player, create video that previews the new addition (which can be included with your press release) or create a video that evaluates the teams' performance at the end of each month (include interviews and professional analysis for flavor).

LIVE POLLS

Live polls are one of the most underutilized and easiest ways to engage your fan base. We poll everything from political preference to what celebrity is best dressed to what we should have for dinner. The evidence is clear; people love to vote when given the chance.

Most digital platforms give you the ability to make a poll via a social media site or your website. Sharing and voting on a simple "question of the week" can grab a lot of interest and interaction. It can also stir debate on your page. Try to search out hot topics within your business or industry that lend themselves to picking a side or forming an opinion. From there you simply need to create the question and possible choices and make the post. Make sure when doing a poll that you share the results. If you wanted to, you could easily base a blog on the results and share your thoughts as the expert.

Aside from asking questions regarding current events, one of the best uses of polls is when you are considering aesthetic changes within your organization. For example, if you are thinking about updating your company logo or your website, show your fan base a few options and let them decide. This is a tremendous way to personally engage your audience while making them feel involved and, at the end of the day, you are the ultimate decision maker so no harm, no foul.

SURVEYS AND QUESTIONNAIRES

Creating a questionnaire and then making a publically available link to it shows your fan base that you clearly value their opinion. Perhaps more importantly, creating surveys can provide you with incredibly valuable information about what is working and failing in the eyes of your fans.

Use an online service that lets you create questionnaires for free or for a small fee. Two of my favorites are SurveyMonkey.com and KwikSurveys.com.

Most surveys are done annually but it's not unheard of to do them twice a year or once a quarter. Gauge what is best for you depending on your goals. Several types of questions can be asked on a survey. Most questions should have predetermined responses along with the option to select "other" and write in an answer when warranted:

Demographic Questions (Answering these should be optional):
- Are you male/female?
- Which age group do you belong to?
- What is your marital status?
- How many children live in your household?

Accessibility Questions:
- How many times did you visit our location in the last year?
- Which platforms do you use to follow our business?

Awareness questions:
- Which of these incentives/sales/themes were you aware of last year?

- When are you most likely to visit our location?
- How long have you used our products/service?
- How much do you typically spend when at our location?

Feedback questions:
- How would you rank your overall experience with our company?
- Which of the following types of promotions would you be interested in receiving via email?
- How interested would you be in purchasing the following types of merchandise at our location?
- How likely are you to recommend our location to a friend?

Open answer questions:
- What would you like to see us do to improve your overall experience?
- How did you first hear about our store/location?
- Any additional comments?

Typically surveys should be available to your audience for 7-14 days. Make sure to alert your fan base through your digital spectrum that the survey is available when you launch and then remind them periodically during its run time to catch any traffic that may not be aware.

When analyzing the answers collected, create a shareable executive summary, highlighting information that stood out along with suggestions. For example, if you find that you have a larger percentage of a certain demographic than you originally thought, write something along the lines of, "35.5% of respondents were aged 18-24, suggesting we have a good foundation of young fans. We can work on creating additional events/social media incentives to tap into this audience." Providing information like this to your internal team will help your company to focus on areas of improvement while also enhancing areas of interest. It will also help to incite creativity that is more specific to your growing audience and will benefit both your business and your fan base.

LIVE Q&A SESSIONS

This is one of my favorite fan tactics as it creates direct interaction between the fans and your organization. Offer your followers the opportunity to join and interact in a live chat with a member of your organization to answer questions.

For example, the Peterborough Phantoms offers fans the opportunity to speak with one of the players through Facebook for one hour. Once a decision is made on a date and time, the promotion of the Q&A event is advertised through social banners. As director of such events, we made it clear that all questions must be in good taste or they would immediately be deleted. When it came time to do the Q&A, we had a member of our media staff create a post welcoming the athlete and our fans to the sessions. From there we allowed the fans to publically start asking questions with our media person moderating the conversation.

The Q&A sessions were a tremendous success. Aside from the chance to get to know their favorite athletes better, the fans thanked the organization for letting them get closer to the team.

CHAPTER 10

INTERACTIVE OPT-IN NEWSLETTER/BUILD A MAILING LIST

This tactic has been heralded by many experts as another "most underutilized tactic" to engage your audience. The creation of an opt-in newsletter is a tremendous way to tap your most engaged fans while providing them with information to share and promotional items to redeem online or at your location.

Newsletters are also an incredibly low-cost and stress-free item to create. The content within your newsletter can be everything from your top news stories for the week, to a calendar of events, to online discounts, to exclusive product launches. Moreover, once you have an established list of readers, you can also send out reminders and "last chance" messages (e.g., Sale Ends Tonight!) if you choose. Just keep in mind that these types of messages should only be done a few times a year to avoid coming across as spam to the reader.

Formatting a basic newsletter is simple. Include:

- Short welcome note

- Links to highlighted content from the week

- Information regarding new product or relevant news

- Photo or video of the week (optional)

- Any business information (address, web and social links, hours of operation, etc.) you want to include

If the above type of newsletter is not your cup of tea, creating a mailing list can also serve as your personal way to connect to readers to share information or do product launches. There is nothing wrong with writing a letter to your faithful, sharing your thoughts on an upcoming product and why you feel it will benefit them. You can provide them with links to your website for more information and a pre-order opportunity.

Announcing the opportunity to sign up for your newsletter can be done several ways. Offer the option on your website in a clearly visible but not intrusive way. For example, you can create a tab or post a sign-up window somewhere on the page that point-blank says, "Sign up for our newsletter to receive the most up-to-date news and offers!" Along with your website announcement, you can periodically alert your social audience that a newsletter is available through other platforms. Do this by providing a link and teasing the information within a specific newsletter (e.g., "We will be offering an exclusive pre-sale opportunity to our newsletter readers tonight! Sign-up using the link below—we'd love to have you!").

Several services are available that allow you to create aesthetically pleasing newsletters via email and provide tracking so you can see what works and what doesn't. Two that I can recommend are Constant Contact and Mail Chimp. ConstantContact.com is a great option if you want to create a template and an aesthetically stimulating newsletter. MailChimp.com is great if you just want to send a basic text-type letter.

CONTENT WITH OTHER COMPANIES (SYNERGY)

Synergy is especially profound for social media. Teaming up with other brands and organizations which mirror your values to share your information is one of the fastest ways to gain new followers and expand your reach.

Searching out and finding potential companies to team up with can be done in several ways. The easiest way is to do a basic online search of your industry and see who pops up. If you work in a popular industry, make sure that you are specific in your search and look for businesses that are around the same size as you or slightly larger, in terms of followers. If you are a small, local company it may or may not be feasible to apply this tactic with a national corporation.

Above all, make sure before reaching out to another company to partner up that you research them extensively. Visit the company's website and look at some of their previous posts and make sure that they are professional and in good taste. If you accidently partner with a company that is controversial, it will affect you as well. Furthermore, if you link your followers to a business that does not provide good service, you damage the trustworthy reputation you have tried so hard to create.

Once you have connected with another company to partner with, teaming up can be done in a few different ways:

Product giveaway: This tactic is usually a win-win for both parties. Offer another channel the opportunity to hold a contest to give one of your products away for free (or vice-versa). You should create a straight-to-the-point photo or banner that will be shared on both your and the other company's pages. In order to win, users must like or follow both your pages (on whichever social networks you'd like) and tag a friend below the post. The next step is to watch your user base grow overnight.

Contests like this can last for a few days but should not go longer than a week. Nightly or midway reminders are encouraged and the incentive should end with the public announcement of the winner.

Mutual info share (shared sponsorship): This method can be used to raise awareness between two channels that are simply looking to tap into each other's audience. Similar to the giveaway, instead of offering your audience free products, you are offering information. This is usually done with two companies that provide different services but whose products work hand in hand. For example, a local gym may partner up with a local sneaker store under the assumption that people who go to the gym need athletic shoes and that people who buy athletic shoes go to the gym. Discuss within your own marketing group what kind of associated businesses might work well with your industry.

Paid endorsements: This approach is one that should be taken only if you have the funds and want to dramatically expand reach quickly. This tactic (which may include a giveaway and/or a mutual info share) would be beneficial for a company that has 5000 followers who wants to approach an account with 50,000+ followers. It is clear that a partnership would be somewhat one sided and some compensation or trade may be in order to make it possible. Explore paid endorsements with a case-by-case mentality and make sure to discuss in depth what the benefits would be, in addition to carefully planning what information you want to the partner to share.

FINAL DOS AND DON'TS

When using any of the above or other techniques, keep in mind the following factors to assure the maximum performance for your efforts. Consider the below when speaking to your audience:

Find the best times to post: The optimal time of day to engage your audience depends on the platform. Your Facebook audience may peak first thing in the morning while your Twitter audience responds mostly at night. Your website traffic may have the most hits on Monday nights, while your Pinterest followers check your wall primarily on weekends. While plenty of guides offer information on when best to publish your information, the truth is tracking an audience is different for everyone. The best method to learn your audience is through experience. Try posting at different times and note your findings. It will not be long before you find your niche for all your networks. This will also help you create an optimal broadcast schedule for each week and maximize your audience.

Be socially aware: Sometimes things happen unexpectedly that take us out of our comfort zone and force us to change our plans. This also affects the digital universe. Whether it be a national disaster, an attack of some sort, the death of a famous person or celebrity, or any other tragedy, make sure you assess how those events affect your audience. Depending on the circumstance, when such disruptive events happen it may be best to suspend any planned posts you have for the day and instead focus on the developing story. For example, the typhoon that ripped through the Philippines in 2013 triggered a major wave of support throughout social media by both individuals and businesses. Can you imagine the social repercussions of being the one organization pushing a product launch when everyone else is fundraising for the displaced and injured?

Simply put, be aware of what is going on around you when you post. While events like the above are rare, they do happen from time to time. If you have already created a post and then realize that something disastrous has happened, make the choice to remove the post and save it for another day.

Always evaluate for good taste: Just because something may be funny to your internal crew does not necessarily mean it will be funny to your audience. A common mistake by businesses when broadcasting is to post "inside jokes" to the public. Make sure when speaking to your audience you always ask the question "Is this for them or for us?" If the answer is the latter make sure to re-evaluate the content before putting it out.

In addition to the "inside joke" examination, make sure that your posts do not accidently offend anyone. As stated in the previous chapter, if you are not sure of the meaning of a word or the validity of some information, don't risk posting it until you have done your research. The consequences of an innocent slip-up could be disastrous for your organization.

Have fun: Above all, when broadcasting to your digital communities, remember to have fun. Take pride in your role as a leader within your industry and make sure that your audience feels that as well. Embrace the concept that attitude reflects leadership and always try to think like a fan when creating, reviewing and sharing your messages with the masses.

IN REVIEW

- With your marketing team, choose and create a healthy mix of techniques and begin to broadcast content to the masses.

- Be aware of what is going on in the world before you post. Posting the wrong message during a national tragedy could be very harmful to how you are perceived publically.

- Attitude reflects leadership. Have fun when communicating!

CONCLUSION

In 1876, a Western Union internal memo stated, "This 'telephone' has too many shortcomings to be seriously considered as a means of communication." In 1939, The New York Times predicted that television would fail because people wouldn't have time to stare at a TV. In 1943, Thomas Watson, chairman of IBM stated, "I think there is a world market for maybe five computers." In 1977, Ken Olson, president of the Digital Equipment Corp commented, "There is no reason anyone would want a computer in their home." In 2003, Steve Jobs said, "The subscription model of buying music is bankrupt." In 2007, Steve Ballmer, CEO of Microsoft said "There's no chance that the iPhone is going to get any significant market share." In 2013 Thorsten Heins, CEO of Blackberry noted, "In five years I don't think there'll be a reason to have a tablet anymore." Although these leaders of various technologies helped to pioneer the communication industry, they all still could not predict the future.

The predictions above all failed to read the changes in the medium just before a major advancement. Make no mistake that we are once again at a precipice that will undoubtedly change how we live. Organizations that aren't preparing to ride the massive wave of new advancements will risk being crushed by its overwhelming force. Athletes practice and hone their skills to be prepared for any situation they may face on the field of play; if businesses want to stay in the game, they should be doing the same.

While the tactics depicted in this book have been proven successful on paper, they would not have been possible without the right teamwork environment. Whether updating or implementing new strategies into your business model, the ability for you and your coworkers to work as a team is paramount to finding success with the items outlined in this book.

I have found that successful brands and teams all share a similar priority system. Above all, the team or organization as a whole comes first. Employees work hard for an organization because they believe in the company and its mission. This is followed by caring for one's teammates or coworkers. When everyone has a common goal they will naturally bond together and set aside major differences to reach that goal. Helping your employees realize they are part of something bigger than themselves is a better motivator than compensation or quitting time.

The group that is the most bonded as a team will find success regardless of how much skill they possess individually. Discovering what motivates each person within your group is the most powerful tool for inspiring results. Some are motivated by money, some by spending time with their family, others simply by a passion for their trade. No matter where motivation is drawn from—as a leader, knowing what drives the people you work with will help you to get the absolute best from them.

The Phantoms' owners enabled our workforce to commit to a common goal while maintaining the trust in each other. As a result, our staff was very accountable for their work. When one person needed help, his or her coworkers surrounded them; no one was allowed to make an unnoticed stumble. Where accountability exists you will also find that when problems arise, instead of dodging them, your staff will try to solve them and improve. When everyone is operating in this way progress is exponentially increased.

Finally, make sure that your workforce has an identity other than just being employees. Begin to refer to your work group as a team. Make sure each individual has background knowledge on the organization you work for. Recreate the passion in the office that your fans feel all the time. Create a circle of trust within your internal team so they can create a trustworthy environment for sponsors, partners, and fans.

If you are a leader that operates from behind a desk, get into the field. If you are in the field, ask—don't tell—your customers what they like or dislike about your service. Also, ask your employees how they feel about your products, services, and company as a whole. Make sure you are listening to them, not just hearing them. Try hard to recognize old-school and outdated sales tactics that are being used and reinvent them. Above all, the first step is to concede that no matter how successful your company might be, it is only for this moment. A company's fate depends on the willingness of its leaders to embrace change, whether technological, organizational, or philosophical.

Remember, just like any leader or team, there will be wins and losses. It's how you and your team respond to each situation and circumstance that matters. Your overall investment in your fans is what will endear these individuals to you both for now and for life.

LEE RECOMMENDS

ONLINE:

Adweek.com – Breaking news in advertising, media, and marketing. Use this as a resource to see what type of marketing is trending.

BusinessWeek.com/technology – Bloomberg Business's top source for tech business news.

Forbes.com – Top site for information for the world's business leaders full of reliable news and financial information.

Google.com – Search the world's information, including webpages, images, videos and more. When in doubt, Google it out!

Gizmodo.com – Source for all up and coming tech news, including apps and gadgets to make life and business more efficient.

Huffpost.com/tech – Get the latest tech industry news. A great source for tech medium and business news and blogs.

MarketingSherpa.com –A firm specializing in tracking all aspects of marketing through research that is catalogued into guides, articles, and reports. Great for case studies to see what works!

Mashable.com – A leading source for news, information, and resources for the Connected Generation. Best resource for news regarding the digital realm.

Statisticbrain.com/tech – A wealth of information, numbers, and statistics. Keep tabs on what technologies are surging and failing which will help in your quest to reach your audience.

Ted.com – "Ideas Worth Spreading" sums up TED's mission. Great resource for speaker videos on a variety of topics.

Wikipedia.com – A free online encyclopedia. Although obvious, it's a great resource for quick fact checks.

WSJ.com/news/technology.com – Blogs and trending news about modern technology. Up to date online coverage of breaking news and current headlines from the US and around the world.

Yahoo! Business and Technology – Helpful online resource for trending information on multiple mediums.

YouTube – Create an account and start subscribing to channels with your interests and potential interests of the audience you're aiming to reach.

PRINT:

Human Bacon: A Man's Guide to Creating an Awesome Personal Brand by Justin Foster

Leaders Eat Last: Why Some Teams Pull Together and Others Don't by Simon Sinek

Freakonomics: A Rogue Economist Explores the Hidden Side of Everything by Steven Levitt and Stephen Dubner

The World is Flat: A Brief History of the 21ˢᵗ Century by Thomas Friedman

The Leadership Challenge: How to Make Extraordinary Things Happen in Organizations by Barry Posner and James Kouzes

Working in Sync: How Eleven Dartmouth Athletes Propelled Their College Sports Experience into Professional Excellence by Whit Mitchell

Eleven Rings: The Soul of Success by Phil Jackson

VIDEO:

Downloaded – A documentary that follows the rise and fall of Napster and its effect on technology trends and society.

THINK LIKE A FAN

Freakonomics – Movie based on the hit book that forces you think outside of the box about financial and economic trends.

Mark Cuban: Bloomberg Game Changers – Chronicles the backstory of major billionaire businessperson and entrepreneur.

Steve Jobs: Just One More Thing – Documentary on the incredible visionary's life and impacts on society.

Something Ventured – Film that follows some of the top investors in technology.

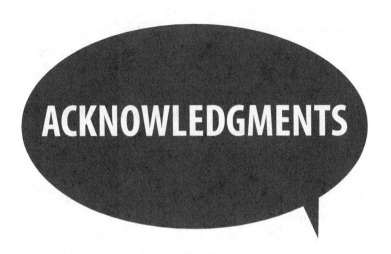

ACKNOWLEDGMENTS

I was blessed and privileged to have so many motivators and believers throughout the writing process. Like athletics, writing is an endurance test and I would not have been able to finish the race if it wasn't for the friends, family and colleagues mentioned in this section.

First and foremost is my wife Janet. We both have extremely busy lives and this project is not something that could have been achieved without your blessing and continued support. I am tremendously proud to be able to call myself your husband and friend. Our family is the most important thing in my life and I thank God everyday for allowing us to find each other. You are my home—I love you!

To my son Logan, you have been a blessing! Some of our friends call you "the happiest baby alive" and they are right. I cannot tell you how many times I have taken a break from writing to peek over my laptop to check on you only to see you smiling back at me. Thank you for being such a great little boy; I am not sure I could have done this otherwise!

Mom and Dad, you have always supported all my ventures in life including this one. I would not have gotten to this point professionally if not for your love and encouragement. You have set an example for me that I hope to share with my children. Parents often say they are proud of their kids—I am proud to be your kid!

Alan, my brother, I have told you countless times that you set a foundation for me growing up. This project is yet another result that stems from the example you set for me. I love you very much (despite your being a Redskins fan) and look forward to watching our children and families grow together.

To my best friend Stacy Rosales Granara, you are glowing beacon of hope and support not just with this project but also within my life. Whether our conversations were about word placement and relevance in the book, pop culture, sports, reminiscing about "IHOP" therapy sessions in our mid-twenties or a "wake up call" to reset my thought process—they always motivated me to write to the best of my ability. More than anyone, this book was possible because of you. I am lucky to have you in my life and look forward to seeing what else we can accomplish together!

I often credit my undergraduate program at Montclair State University with giving me the tools to be prepared for the professional world. This situation is no different. To Dr. David Sanders and Patricia Piroh, my professors, advisors and now friends—many of the concepts in this book stem from your lessons to me as a young adult. I am always amazed how often I reference lessons and advice shared by you at the DuMont in all facets of my life. Carpe Diem!

This book is largely based on my Masters' Thesis from the Sports Management program at Drexel University. I can pinpoint the exact moment—sitting in front of my computer doing a classroom response—which the fundamental idea for the book came to me. That idea blossomed due to the guidance of three people: Dr. Amy Giddings (my thesis advisor), Heather Blackburn (Director of Students), and the late David O'Brien—who served as Program Director during my time at school. Thank you for encouraging and inspiring me to attempt something as daunting as a book! I hope that it will serve the program well in future years.

I must also thank the Peterborough Phantoms Ice Hockey Organization, my British family, for trusting my plans and vision. Many of the concepts in this book would be just concepts had you not let me implement them. Big thanks to team owners Rob and Sue Housden and Dave and Jo Lane. I also must thank the organization's Director of Hockey Jon Kynaston and the team's equipment manager Callum Owen who opened the door for me to join the team. And another big thanks to the best media crew anyone could ask for: Carrie Buckman, Matt Cavalieri, Dan Breen, Ian Offers, Tom Scott, and Dave Tudman. I will forever be grateful for your patience, trust and willingness to follow my lead—even though I am American!

I get by with a little help from my friends. I must point out several people who made contributions to this project either by providing me with information, engaging me in conversation, and/or supporting me as a friend! Elaine Rand—your editing work on the original thesis from which this book is based is a large reason it was able to find success. I could not write enough words to thank you for your time and dedication to my writing! Dan Moffitt— During a rough patch in my professional career you gave me one of the simplest but most influential pieces of advice I have every received. I can still hear your voice on the phone saying, "Dare to be great". I have followed that advice every day since and continue to strive to do so! Bob Pinard—your never-ending quest for knowledge was infectious to me—thanks for making learning fun again. Tyler Day and Jenna Barker—whether it was at the rink, over a drink, or via Internet link—you have been great friends to me. Tom Moldenhauer—thanks for always being there at 1 AM when I was struggling to stay awake (and thanks for your service to this country!). Jon Blevins—Classmate at Drexel and friend, thanks for always being so positive and encouraging when it comes to the world of sports. Chris Kibui—I cannot thank you enough for believing in my ideas and implementing them within your ventures. Ray Carsillo—watching you strive to accomplish your dreams has inspired me. We run together brother! Bill, Samantha and (my beautiful God-daugher) Nina Weisel—You remain the couple and family that I most admire. Thanks for being family to me.

To the creative team at Aloha Publishing—Jennifer Regner for your proofreading insights, Fusion Creative Works for your on-point design of the cover and book— thank you for making this book the best it could be.

Finally to Maryanna Young and Hannah Cross at Aloha Publishing—I cannot begin to tell you how much I have enjoyed the process of working with you. Aside from taking a chance on an unknown writer/hockey coach/media guy that currently lives across the Atlantic. The confidence you have instilled in me as both an author and speaker is a gift that I only can hope to repay one day. I have never told either of you this but when I was eight years old I was asked to write down on what I wanted to be when I grew up— the answer put down was "a writer." I have been blessed in my life to have several jobs that I have enjoyed—but you have literally made my dream job as a child a reality. Thank you for that! I look forward to a bright future of friendship and working together!

ABOUT THE AUTHOR

Lee Elias's credentials are rooted in sports, marketing, and management. He is a graduate of Montclair State University in Upper Montclair, New Jersey with a B.A. in Broadcasting and a postgraduate degree from Drexel University in Philadelphia, Pennsylvania, with a M.S. in Sports Management. He has built a unique skill set through his professional experience.

His most recent work has been in England with the Peterborough Phantoms Ice Hockey Club in the dual role of Player Development Coach and Game Operations and Content Production Manager. In his first year with the coaching staff the Phantoms won the 2015 Playoff Championship of the English Premier Ice Hockey League (EPIHL). Lee is also partial owner and Director of Business Development and Marketing with HockeyWrapAround.com.

Lee's other sports work experiences includes serving the National Hockey League as the Coordinator of the NHL Network during its first season in the USA while simultaneously being General Manager and Head Coach of the Montclair State University Ice Hockey team. Lee also worked as a Camera Director for the New York Rangers and New York Knicks at Madison Square Garden. Beyond that, he served as a Production Specialist with the Pensacola Blue Wahoos (Cincinnati Reds AA) during their inaugural season.

In addition to his sports experience, in 2010 Lee was hired by LocalEdge, a Division of Hearst Media Services. With the company he helped small-to-medium-sized businesses create digital plans focusing on search engine optimization, search engine marketing, social media marketing, and mobile marketing, among other solutions. Lee also was responsible for development of new consultants, and assisting with product development, marketing, product expertise, and public speaking.

Lee currently resides in England with his wife Janet, who is a physician, their son, Logan, and their two dogs, Philly and Chewy, and cat, Yoda.

ABOUT THE CO-AUTHOR

Stacy Rosales Granara began her professional career at Procter & Gamble, where she represented billion-dollar healthcare brand franchises and cultivated skills in sales, marketing, project management, people management, training, and mentoring. She later joined Strategic Experiential Group, where she fell in love with marketing and events. It was there that she produced, managed, and worked luxury branded events, and learned the ins and outs of experiential marketing, brand promotion, and program activations. In the last few years, Stacy has taken her passions and applied her expertise in business to pursue her dream career, focusing on health, wellness, yoga, sports, and other creative pursuits. She is a Certified Personal Trainer, Registered Yoga Instructor, and Board Certified Holistic Health Coach. She works with a number of companies in Colorado Springs, Colorado, and works one-on-one with clients all over the country to provide everything from personal training, private yoga instruction, and one-on-one health coaching, to consulting in the areas of marketing and business/program development. She specializes in offering a holistic, customized approach to her work rooted in support, education, accountability, and motivation.

Stacy is inspired daily by those around her trailblazing the pursuit of happiness. She looks up to Richard Branson and Rob Dyrdek for their fearless and relentless quests for fun and innovation in their business ventures. She admires fellow leaders who embody servant leadership and lead-by-example philosophies, and values quality, learning, creativity, diversity, innovation, and fun!

Stacy's personal passions include food and nutrition, yoga, sports, travel, and great conversations and laughter with her friends and family all over this big, beautiful world. She currently resides in Colorado Springs, Colorado with her husband, Jimmy, a Staff Sergeant in the United States Air Force, their Russian Blue feline, Sammie, and their Miniature Dachshund, McLovin.

FAN TACTICS

Lee Elias, renowned coach of brands, companies, and teams, shows you how organizational leaders can use existing resources around them in order to build a culture of fans who are intensely loyal to their brand and are willing to talk about it.

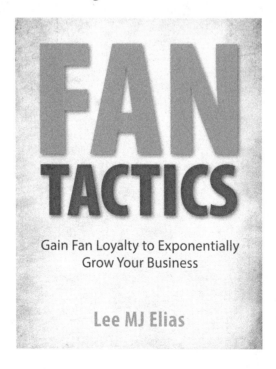

FAN TACTICS

Gain Fan Loyalty to Exponentially
Grow Your Business

Lee MJ Elias

I work with business leaders to discover, create and evolve communication within their organizations using the spirit and culture of a professional sports organization.

I'd love to hear from you. Visit my website www.leemjelias.com or email leemjelias@gmail.com.

 Facebook /leeelias   YouTube /leemjelias   Twitter @leemjelias

 Instagram leemjelias   GooglePlus Lee Elias